P9-DXI-920

50627

PSYCHOLOGICAL ISSUES

VOL. II, No. 4	1960	MONOGRAPH 8

PERSONALITY ORGANIZATION IN COGNITIVE CONTROLS AND INTELLECTUAL ABILITIES

by

RILEY W. GARDNER
DOUGLAS N. JACKSON
SAMUEL J. MESSICK

Gellert Memorial Library
St. Patrick's Seminary & University
Menlo Park, CA 94025
library.stpsu.edu

INTERNATIONAL UNIVERSITIES PRESS, INC.
227 West 13 Street   •   New York 11, N. Y.

Copyright 1960, by International Universities Press, Inc.

BF
698
.G29
1960

EDITORIAL STATEMENT

In the last twenty-five years psychoanalytic interest has ranged far beyond psychopathology and the therapeutic process. As Heinz Hartmann has put it, "We no longer doubt that psychoanalysis can claim to be a *general* psychology in the broadest sense of the word." The Editors of *Psychological Issues* believe that a new kind of journal is needed which will publish diversified source materials for a general psychoanalytic theory of behavior.

The Editors believe that relevant contributions can come from experimental studies as well as from clinical ones, from controlled developmental studies as well as from the genetic explorations of psychoanalytic therapy, and that investigations carried out without any concern for psychoanalysis may nevertheless contribute to the theory. In *Psychological Issues,* readers who are particularly concerned with psychoanalytic theory will therefore come into contact with important research not ordinarily presented in psychoanalytic journals.

Although the Editors have an important commitment to the advancement of psychoanalytic theory, they will try to make *Psychological Issues* interesting and relevant to investigators of all theoretical persuasions in psychology, psychiatry, and related fields. By selecting only monographs which confront fundamental psychological issues or that contain fresh and penetrating observations of phenomena, the Editors hope that the journal will be a meeting ground for all serious investigators of behavior.

The Board will consider only contributions submitted on invitation. There is at present no provision for consideration of unsolicited manuscripts.

Psychological Issues will publish four monographs per volume. These will appear at irregular intervals. The journal is sold mainly by subscription ($10.00 per volume). Single issues are purchasable and are priced individually.

Subscriptions should be sent directly to the publisher, International Universities Press, Inc., 227 West 13 Street, New York 11, N. Y. Editorial correspondence should be sent to the Editor, Dr. George S. Klein, Research Center for Mental Health, New York University, Washington Square, New York 3, N. Y.

POLICY ANNOUNCEMENT

Psychological Issues' declared purpose of publishing four mono-graphs in a calendar year has proved to be unrealistic. The me-chanics of processing long manuscripts, each posing different problems for the careful editing to which all monographs without exception are subjected, and the rewriting required in some in-stances, have made it difficult to adhere to the standard journal practice of a fixed publication date.

Rather than retreat from its editorial standards to conform to the four-issues-per-year policy, *Psychological Issues* has decided to make its publication dates more flexible. It will issue its unit of four monographs over an eighteen-month period without changing its subscription policy: the subscription rate will continue to cover four issues. For bibliographic listings, the four monographs will be dated within the same calendar year.

It is our hope that this change will reduce the instances of an announced publication date proving unreliable, with its incon-venience to readers and embarrassment to the editors. For earlier such instances we offer sincere apologies.

CONTENTS

Preface   ix

1 STRUCTURE AND STYLE IN COGNITIVE ORGANIZATION   1

The Cognitive Control Principles   2
   Psychoanalytic Theory and Cognitive Control Principles   4
   The Stability of Cognitive Control Principles   7
   Sex-Linked Differences in Cognitive Control Principles   7
   Cognitive Controls and Cognitive Styles   8
The Intellectual Abilities   9
The Question of Relationships Between Cognitive Control
   Principles and Intellectual Abilities   10

2 METHOD   13

The Sample of Subjects   13
Procedure   13
   Control Principle Tests   14
   Intellectual Ability Tests   15
   Additional Scores   16
Analysis of the Data   17

3 FIELD-ARTICULATION, CONSTRICTED-FLEXIBLE CONTROL, AND
   SPATIAL RELATIONS AND ORIENTATION   18

The Field-Articulation Principle   18
Field-Articulation As Selectiveness of Attention:
   Theoretical Considerations   23
   Field-Articulation and the Psychoanalytic View of Attention   24
   Field-Articulation in Relation to Piaget's Studies of Attention   28
   A Gestalt-Psychological View of Perceptual Articulation   30
   Summary of the View of Field-Articulation Guiding This Study   31
Field-Articulation and Constricted-Flexible Control   32
The Flexibility of Closure Ability   32
The Spatial Relations and Orientation Ability   33
Hypotheses   34

v

Tests and Measures of Field-Articulation 35
    Embedded Figures Test 35
    Rod and Frame Test 37
Tests and Measures of Constricted-Flexible Control 38
    Color-Word Test 38
    Size Estimation Test 41
Tests and Measures of Flexibility of Closure 42
    Concealed Figures Test 42
    Designs Test 43
Tests and Measures of Spatial Relations and Orientation 44
    Spatial Orientation Test 44
    Cards Test 46
Results 47
Discussion of Results 51

4 FIELD-ARTICULATION AND THE ABILITIES OF VERBAL KNOWL-
    EDGE, GENERAL REASONING, AND IDEATIONAL FLUENCY 55

The Verbal Knowledge Ability 56
The General Reasoning Ability 57
The Ideational Fluency Ability 58
Hypotheses 59
Tests and Measures of the Three Abilities 59
    Wide Range Vocabulary Test (Verbal Knowledge) 59
    Mathematics Aptitude Test (General Reasoning) 61
    Thing Categories Test (Ideational Fluency) 63
Results 64
Discussion of Results 66

5 LEVELING-SHARPENING, FIELD-ARTICULATION, AND THE
    ASSOCIATIVE MEMORY ABILITY 67

The Leveling-Sharpening Principle 67
Leveling-Sharpening and Field-Articulation As Determinants of
    Learning and Recall 69
The Associative Memory Ability 70
Hypotheses 71
Tests and Measures of Leveling-Sharpening 71
    The Schematizing Test 71
Tests and Measures of Associative Memory 73
    Picture-Number Test 73
    Word-Number Test 75
Results 75
Discussion of Results 77

6 EQUIVALENCE RANGE, FIELD-ARTICULATION, AND THE
       INDUCTION AND DEDUCTION ABILITIES   79

   Concept Formation and the Equivalence-Range Principle   79
   The Induction and Deduction Abilities   82
   Hypotheses   83
   Tests and Measures of Equivalence Range   84
       Object Sorting Test   84
       Size Constancy Test   85
   Tests and Measures of Induction   87
       Letter Grouping Test   87
       Marks Test   89
   Tests and Measures of Deduction   91
       False Premises Test   91
       Reasoning Test   92
   Results   94
   Analysis of Levels of Abstraction   101
   Discussion of Results   101

7 INDIVIDUAL CONSISTENCIES IN COGNITION   104

   A Factor Analysis of Correlations Between the Two
       Batteries of Tests   105
   A Factor Analysis of All the Correlations for the
       Two Batteries of Tests   107
   Discussion of the Factor-Analytic Results   112

8 THEORETICAL IMPLICATIONS OF THE STUDY   114

9 THE STUDY IN BRIEF   121

   APPENDICES

   A. Intercorrelations of Forty Scores   124
   B. Results of Interbattery Analysis   129
   C. Results of Principal Components Analysis   132

   Bibliography   141

   About the Authors   150

PREFACE

The study described in this monograph was made possible by research grants to The Menninger Foundation's Perception Project by the National Institute of Mental Health, Public Health Service. The larger exploration of cognitive control principles of which the present study is one part was supported by Research Grant M-1182. A generous supplement to this grant by the Public Health Service provided funds for the extension of this study to include certain intellectual abilities. Dr. Philip S. Holzman was then director of The Menninger Foundation's Perception Project, and he did much to make this study possible. Dr. Richard S. Siegal, also a member of this research group, contributed to the testing required to obtain measures of both the control principles and the abilities involved.

Dr. Gardner Murphy, director of research at The Menninger Foundation, made helpful suggestions about the first draft of this report and has consistently supported and encouraged the explorations of cognitive controls which led to the present study. Drs. Robert Wallerstein, Howard Shevrin, Robert Long, and Wayne Holtzman provided helpful comments on all or part of the manuscript. Miss Lolafaye Coyne performed much of the scoring of control-principle tests and many other aspects of the statistical work.

The conception of cognitive control and its experimental exemplification both owe much to the editor of this series, Dr. George S. Klein. Special reference must also be made here to the work of Dr. David Rapaport. His pioneer exposition, with Drs. Merton Gill and Roy Schafer, of the processes involved in responses to intelligence tests served as a general model for the rationales of intellectual ability tests developed for the present study. Linked to the rationales developed earlier for the cognitive control tests, these tentative process interpretations provided the predictive framework around which the study was organized.

Funds for one of the factor analyses included in the present study were provided by the Educational Testing Service, Princeton, New Jersey. Dr. David R. Saunders helped to make this analysis possible. Dr. Ledyard R Tucker offered valuable advice in our application of his interbattery method of factor analysis.

1

STRUCTURE AND STYLE IN
COGNITIVE ORGANIZATION

The study described in this monograph was designed to explore
relationships between two general classes of variables, *cognitive
control principles* and *intellectual abilities*. Our purpose in this
venture was twofold: (a) to illustrate that these two domains of
cognitive organization have commonalities which can be conceptualized within a single set of principles of personality organization; and (b) to explore several hypotheses concerning relations
between particular control principles and abilities.

This chapter will be devoted to an introductory discussion of the
theoretical and empirical foundations of the two classes of variables,
cognitive control principles and intellectual abilities, and a consideration of possible relations between them.

Chapter 2 contains a description of the method and design of the
study, a list of the tests and scores used to represent the cognitive
controls and intellectual abilities dealt with, and a brief discussion
of the use of factor analysis both as a means of testing hypotheses
and as an exploratory tool.

Chapter 3 deals with the major specific hypotheses of the present
study, which concern the *field-articulation* principle and the intellectual abilities of *flexibility of closure* and *spatial relations and
orientation*. The interpretation of the field-articulation principle
by Gardner et al. (1959) is elaborated upon. This interpretation
deals in part with the important studies of Witkin and his co-
workers (e.g., 1954, 1959), whose findings highlight the usefulness
of careful, systematic, and extensive explorations of individual differences in cognition. The empirical work that initially led us to
hypothesize relationships between this dimension of cognitive control

1

and intellectual abilities was done by Jackson (1955, 1957), who found significant correlations between measures of intellectual ability (largely representing verbal and general reasoning factors) and performance in Witkin's Embedded Figures Test. Since the interpretation of the field-articulation principle concerns individual strategies of attending, connections to Piaget's extensive studies of the developmental emergence of schemata guiding attention are spelled out in somewhat greater detail than in related reports (e.g., Gardner et al., 1959; Gardner, in press). Like Chapters 4 to 6, this chapter includes new rationales for the ability tests and a discussion of correlational results bearing upon the specific hypotheses dealt with.

Chapter 4 describes an exploration of the generality of the field-articulation principle by an examination of its relations to the abilities of *verbal knowledge, general reasoning,* and *ideational fluency.*

Chapter 5 contains a description of the *leveling-sharpening* control principle and describes an extension of studies that show the relationship of field-articulation on the one hand, and leveling-sharpening on the other, to different aspects of learning and recall.

Chapter 6 deals with the possibility that the *equivalence range* and field-articulation control principles are differentially related to the *induction* and *deduction* abilities.

Chapter 7 contains a description of two applications of factor analysis, detailed interpretations of the major factors obtained, and a discussion of their meaning.

Chapter 8 is focused upon general implications of the study. Some of the major questions that remain are spelled out and suggestions are offered concerning the solution of these problems.

Chapter 9 is a brief résumé of the study.

THE COGNITIVE CONTROL PRINCIPLES

In the context of recent developments in psychoanalytic ego psychology, cognitive control principles have been conceived of as ego "structures" which are essential attributes of personality organization and control certain aspects of adaptive behavior. They are thought to guide the expression of drive in response to particular classes of adaptive requirement. Thus they are presumed to emerge in the course of development as *mediating* structures that take their form from drives, from constitutional characteristics of the relevant ego apparatuses, and from the adaptive problems the individual has encountered. These principles of cognitive organization have been used to account for individual consistencies in response to a wide variety of test situations.

Various cognitive control principles have been formulated on the basis of the theoretical work of G. S. Klein and his co-workers (e.g., Klein, 1949a, 1949b, 1951, 1956, 1958; Klein and Schlesinger, 1949; Holzman and Klein, 1956) and experimental studies by Klein and Schlesinger (1951); Klein, Gardner, and Schlesinger (in press); Klein (1954); Holzman (1954); Holzman and Klein (1954); Holzman and Gardner (1959; in press); Gardner (1953, 1959, in press); Gardner, Holzman, Klein, Linton, and Spence (1959); Gardner and Lohrenz (1960); Gardner and Long (1960a, b, c, d; in press; in preparation, a, b, c); and others.

Gardner (1960) has summarized research on the five major control principles defined thus far: leveling-sharpening, equivalence range, scanning, constricted-flexible control, and field-articulation. Relations between controls were first explored by Gardner et al. (1959) and later by Gardner (in press) and Gardner and Long (in preparation, c). In past and current studies of these controls, major interest has centered on the following: (a) development of process rationales for the controls and the tests used to sample them; (b) the realms of operation of the controls; (c) relations between drive states and controls; (d) relations between defenses and controls. These studies indicate that each of the controls isolated thus far is evident in a variety of situations which are linked by generically similar adaptive conditions and requirements. These principles of reality contact are, in adults, relatively stable and enduring aspects of cognition. They are, however, capable of notable temporary variations under the impact of intense need, anxiety, preoccupation, etc. Much further work is needed in the area of relations between drive states and controls. Now that a group of stable controls has been tentatively isolated, such questions can be pursued more vigorously and with greater clarity than was possible at the time (1956-1957) the data of the present study were collected.

Psychoanalytic Theory and Cognitive Control Principles

As noted above, and as pointed out earlier by Klein (1954) and Gardner, Holzman, Klein, Linton, and Spence (1959), psychoanalytic theory may provide a framework in which to conceive of cognitive controls as general principles of ego organization which modulate the expression of drives in particular classes of adaptive situations. This view of cognitive controls owes much to Freud, who early conceived of mental structures as enduring arrangements of processes, as exemplified in his formulations concerning defensive structures. The control-principle conception is also linked to the recent developments in ego psychology represented in theoretical works by Hartmann, Kris, Loewenstein, and Rapaport.

Attempts to define cognitive control principles have also been influenced by the pioneer efforts of Rapaport and others (see Rapaport, 1942a, 1946, 1952; Rapaport, Gill, and Schafer, 1945, 1946; Schafer, 1948, 1954) to conceptualize performances in *clinical* psychological tests in terms of certain aspects of psychoanalytic theory.

Following the early emphasis in psychoanalytic theorizing on unconscious processes and the special set of "rules" governing primary-process functions, more and more attention has been paid to the secondary processes that channel drives in the service of adaptation. Following Freud's (1915a) original description of secondary repression, and his later descriptions of other counter-cathectic functions, a major portion of interest in these relatively autonomous structures (see, for example, Anna Freud, 1937; Rapaport, 1951a, 1951c, 1957; Hartmann, 1956) centered upon the mechanisms of defense. The cognitive control principles we are concerned with here have been considered analogous to the defenses in their place in psychoanalytic theory (see Gardner et al., 1959), but are thought to serve different (nondefensive) purposes and to have different antecedents (Klein, 1954; Gardner et al., 1959; Holzman and Gardner, 1959; Holzman, 1960).

The general concept of "psychic structure" (originally outlined by Freud in his "Project for a Scientific Psychology," written in 1895) may help to distinguish the control principles from the constructs used in discussions of intellectual abilities. The concept was developed by Freud in a number of his later works and has received extensive consideration and elaboration by Hartmann (e.g., 1950), Hartmann and Kris (1945), Hartmann, Kris, Loewenstein (1946), Rapaport (1957), and others. Hartmann's (1939) development of the concept of automatization and Rapaport's (1951b, 1958) discussion of the *relative* autonomy of the ego from both drives and reality, for example, are rooted in the basic assumption that psychological development implies the emergence of structures that "partly control, and are partly controlled by, the underlying organizations from which they emerged" (Rapaport, 1951b, p. 115). The structures called "defenses" imply the existence of conflict. The structures called "cognitive control principles" may not. In fact, the operation of cognitive controls has at times been inferred from individual consistencies in cognitive behaviors that are in no obvious way related to conflict.

Hartmann (e.g., 1939) has emphasized that the inborn apparatuses (e.g., perception, memory) which subserve the ego's defensive and controlling functions comprise a "conflict-free" sphere of ego functioning, although the uses to which these apparatuses are put are in part determined by conflicts. Holzman and Gardner (1959) have confirmed a relationship between the leveling-sharpening control principle and the defense of repression and have speculated that extreme leveling may reflect a basic characteristic of the memory apparatus and its employment that provides a necessary but insufficient condition for the emergence of repression as a predominant defense. Gardner et al. (1959) and Gardner and Long (in preparation, b) have shown that the control principle called *scanning,* which concerns the characteristic extensiveness with which individuals sample external fields of stimulation or internal fields of ideas, may be linked to the defense of isolation. In both cases, persons extreme in their employment of these defenses are at one extreme in respect to the control-principle dimension. But in both cases, a number of persons at the extreme of the control dimensions are not extreme in the defense. Such findings have led Holzman and Gardner (1959) to speculate that cognitive controls may be general principles of cognitive organization which emerge early in development and which may serve as preconditions for the emergence of particular defenses. Repression may be a natural defense for a person generally prone to gross interaction between percepts and memories (including unconscious, drive-organized memories as well as memories organized by higher levels of conceptualization). These and related questions require much further exploration before definitive answers can be given. It is also apparent that defense and control may be different structures formed to serve different *intentions*. Or it may be that further studies will suggest a level of cognitive organization superior to both control and defense.

The emphasis noted above upon the concept of structure as a key to understanding the place of adaptive behaviors in personality organization separates psychoanalytic theory from many other theories (see Rapaport, 1950a), but places it directly in line with recent theoretical emphasis upon the adaptive nature of behavior. Piaget's conception of schemata emerging from the interaction of assimilation (internalization of the external world) and accommodation (adjustment of behavior to conform to external conditions), for example, is in some ways closely related to these developments in psychoanalytic ego psychology. The progression from egocentric to reality-oriented assimilation which Piaget describes (e.g., 1936), with its counterparts in the development of schemata that govern thought functioning, is closely related to Freud's early (e.g., 1900, 1911) distinction between the consequences for thought functioning of (a) unmediated primary-process behaviors serving the pleasure principle and (b) mediated behaviors serving the reality principle. Anthony (1957), Wolff (1960), and others have recently focused attention on relations between the theoretical systems developed by Freud and Piaget. Gardner et al. (1959), Gardner (1959, in press), and Gardner and Long (1960a, 1960b) have pointed to similar links between Piaget's theories and the conception of cognitive control.

It is important to note here the usefulness of the control-principle construct in understanding the effects of needs upon cognition. Holzman and Klein (1956) and Klein (1958) have noted, for example, that current theories of perception vary widely when directed toward such questions. At one extreme, it has been assumed that perception is plastic and molds itself in conformance to the individual's momentary need states. Klein (1954) has shown, however, that a cognitive control principle can determine the effects of a need state upon cognition. In similar states of need, persons with different mediating structures differ in their perception of need-related objects. Thus, momentary needs do not have direct effects upon cognition. The particular organization of adaptive properties that characterizes the individual (see Klein, 1949a; Holzman and Klein, 1956; Gardner, 1959) mediates the expression of the need in percepts, ideas, or other cognitive "products." Klein (1958) has expanded and elaborated this aspect of control in a recent paper.

As Holzman and Klein (1956) have pointed out, relatively autonomous secondary structures, including cognitive control principles, in some ways become "motives" in themselves. The exercise of mediating structures may in itself entail gratification, as when one seeks out particular kinds of tasks, or pursues a particular hobby that allows free expression to his particular organization of adaptive propensities.

In summary, the cognitive control principles are conceived of as structures leading to the kind of "constancy and reliability" in behavior referred to by Rapaport (1951a). It is assumed that they are activated primarily by adaptive requirements, rather than by conflict, and that they represent a distinguishable class of ego characteristics.

The Stability of Cognitive Control Principles

Witkin et al. (e.g., 1954) have provided evidence of the persistence of the cognitive control principle referred to here as field-articulation. Gardner and Long (in press) have recently demonstrated satisfactory reliabilities for other control-principle scores over periods of up to three years in young adults. Thus there seems to be clear evidence that cognitive controls are enduring aspects of adult personality organization. Questions concerning the emergence of these stable patterns of control in childhood require further developmental studies of the kind done for field-articulation measures by Witkin and his co-workers (see Witkin et al., 1954, 1959).

Sex-Linked Differences in Cognitive Control Principles

As noted by Witkin et al. (e.g., 1954), Gardner et al. (1959), and others, women are generally less adept than men at the kinds of adaptive tasks used to measure field-articulation. The control is obviously present, however, in both sexes. Other control principles have not provided clear evidence of sex-linked differences. The study by Gardner et al. of relationships between various controls did, however, raise the question of different *patterns* of controls in men and women. Assuming that the latter tentative observations might be a function of the small samples of men and women employed by Gardner et al., Gardner (1959; in press) and Gardner and Long (in preparation, b, c) have shown, for example, that individual consistencies in the scanning control can be observed as easily in the adaptive behaviors of women (for whom no scanning factor appeared in the earlier study) as in those of men when larger samples are used and more effective isolation of the relevant aspects of behavior is achieved. The possibility of sex differences in the *patterning* of controls remains, however, and dictated the use of only one sex in the present study.

Cognitive Controls and Cognitive Styles

Klein (1958) and Gardner et al. (1959) have suggested that patterns or arrangements of individual controls may comprise superordinate ego structures that can be designated as *cognitive styles*. It may be that molar aspects of individual differences in other areas of personality organization are linked primarily to *styles* rather than to individual controls. Thus, predictions to certain general aspects of interpersonal relations may ideally be based upon knowledge that a particular leveler, for example, is also a limited scanner, a poor field-articulator, of broad equivalence range, of constricted rather than flexible control, and intolerant of unrealistic experiences, rather than upon the limited knowledge that he is a leveler.

The fact that several control principles have appeared to be quite independent of each other in studies to date means that a leveler may be high or low in habitual extensiveness of scanning, etc., so that knowledge of his *pattern* of controls adds to our understanding of his cognitive organization.

Some of the individual cognitive control principles formulated thus far have implications for different segments of "intelligent" behaviors (see Gardner et al., 1959, Ch. 12). This fact, and the very large numbers of subjects needed to study patterns of control—cognitive styles—led to the formulation of predictions concerning *particular* control dimensions and clusters of ability tests in the present study. No attempt was made with the present sample of only sixty-three persons to explore relations between the stylistic level and either first- or second-order ability factors.

The Intellectual Abilities

Factor-analytic studies of intelligence have generally been carried out within one of two theoretical frameworks: (a) that of Spearman and his followers, who long devoted their efforts to showing the presence of a general, or "g," factor, plus more specific factors; and (b) that of investigators pursuing multiple-factor assumptions. For the most part, British factor analysts followed the former assumption and American factor analysts the latter. Vernon (1950) and Guilford (1956, 1959a, 1959b) are among those who have recently pointed out that no consistent "g" factor appears from study to study and who have suggested that the multiple-factor approach may be on firmer ground. Vernon (1950) has offered cogent arguments for a hierarchical conception of major and minor abilities.

Our discussion of intellectual abilities rests directly upon the work of Thurstone, who not only pioneered in the exploration of these abilities (1938) but anticipated the discovery of more general "perceptual attitudes" in his later (1944) study of perception. Although refined in subsequent studies, the *flexibility of closure* ability discussed in Chapter 3 is essentially a factor Thurstone isolated. Thurstone did not organize his factorial study of perception around specific hypotheses concerning the individual consistencies he might observe, and thus performed a strictly empirical study based upon commonly used laboratory procedures. He was alert, however, to the possibility that response dispositions more general than those usually attributed to abilities might be elicited by the procedures he selected.

The explorations of intellectual abilities by Thurstone and later workers who employed factor analysis in studies of intelligence have been notable for the care with which repeatedly appearing factors have been isolated. Some of the correlated abilities considered in the present study have appeared in more than forty factor-analytic studies. Verbal abilities are among the most commonly observed of these variables. Other abilities are assumed to represent various aspects of reasoning, learning, perception, spatial orientation, the capacity to visualize spatial relations, and a variety of other relatively specific aspects of cognition. A large number of ability studies was summarized and the results codified by French (1951). Tests and measures representing various abilities underwent further winnowing in the hands of a group of experts on ability studies. This group chose ability factors that were clearly evident in a number of previous studies and compiled a "Kit" of key tests and measures of each ability (French, 1954). All the ability tests used in the present study were drawn from this "Kit."

In contrast to Thurstone's study of perceptual behaviors, most studies of intellectual abilities have employed only paper-and-pencil tests. The "Kit" compiled by French (1954) and others contains only such procedures. The demand for group tests ideal for the collection of large bodies of data amenable to factor analysis seems to have contributed to the preservation of this arbitrary limitation of the behaviors observed in most ability studies.

At the outset of the present study, it seemed possible that a theory of intelligence which is limited to the current conceptions of intellectual abilities might be inadequate. Although Thurstone (1948) suggested that factor-analytic studies should be designed to test hypotheses concerning psychological processes, some of the ability *concepts* that have emerged from the extensive factor-analytic studies are little more than labels referring to the apparent contents of clusters of paper-and-pencil tests.

THE QUESTION OF RELATIONSHIPS BETWEEN COGNITIVE CONTROL PRINCIPLES AND INTELLECTUAL ABILITIES

Rapaport (1951c, p. 79) has pointed out that the psychoanalytic model "does away with the arbitrary segregation of conation, cognition, and affection." The nature of the complex of constitutional "givens" and environmental influences out of which ego structures arise is such as to preclude the development of cognitive structures that are completely independent of other structures. Thus, the question we posed was not, "How are cognitive control principles (or intellectual abilities) related to personality organization?" but, "What are the most economical ways of conceptualizing the structural aspects of personality organization represented by cognitive control principles and abilities?" This view of the problem—with its demand for consideration of all relevant tests and measures in terms of their psychological rationales—was of primary importance to the study described here.

The general hypothesis that the cognitive structures determining the individual patterns of cognitive control and intellectual ability must in some way be related was also stimulated by Gardner Murphy's (1947) treatment of personality structure and his emphasis upon functional relations between differentiated subsystems.

For the most part, abilities have been studied within their own limited realm of concepts and procedures. Thurstone (1948) pointed, however, to possible links between intellectual abilities and aspects of temperament. Tomkins (1951), Pemberton (1952a, 1952b), Cattell (1955, 1957), and Barratt (1955) are among those who have explored relations between abilities and other aspects of personality organization. Although a limited group of studies, these investigations have important implications for the present study, since the temperament variables associated with the flexibility of closure and spatial abilities are similar to those Witkin has shown to be related to the control principle referred to here as field-articulation. These findings seemed to support the major hypotheses of the present study, which concern links between the field-articulation principle and these two abilities (see Chapter 3).

Fruchter (1954) has referred to a number of studies indicating sex-linked differences in spatial abilities. These differences parallel those observed in the field-articulation principle. Barratt (1955) is among those whose recent findings further confirm the superiority of boys over girls in response to spatial tests.

Developmental curves for spatial abilities may also be roughly parallel to those Witkin (1959) has found for core measures of the field-articulation principle. This fact, too, suggests links between this control principle and certain abilities.

The fact that cognitive control principles have been formulated to account for a *variety* of structural aspects of the ego made it clear in advance that not all these principles need necessarily be related to intellectual abilities. For example, the principle called *tolerance for unrealistic experiences* could be expected to find little or no representation in the reference tests from which ability measures were derived in the present study.[1] Nor was it obvious that the *scanning* principle would be related to abilities. It is important to note here that control principles were not formulated to account simply for success or achievement. Although in some circumstances it may be helpful to be a sharpener, in others it may be more useful to be a leveler. Although extreme intolerance for unrealistic experiences may imply a rigid coordination with external criteria of reality that is useful for some purposes, it implies an undue, and perhaps "brittle," autonomy from drives and their lower-order thought derivatives which could act as a severe limitation on creativity, "psychological-mindedness," empathy, warmth in interpersonal relationships, etc. On the other hand, the field-articulation principle —although already shown by Witkin, Gardner et al., Crutchfield, Woodworth, and Albrecht (1958), and others to be a general principle of cognitive organization—includes skills that can be considered abilities. The leveling-sharpening principle, too, may have implications for success or failure in certain kinds of situations, particularly those requiring learning and recall, although the studies of this principle also reveal its much more general relevance to cognitive organization.

Because of the obvious overlap of behaviors sampled in laboratory tests of *field-articulation* and tests of the abilities called *flexibility of closure* and *spatial relations and orientation,* the major predictions of the present study dealt with relationships between these variables (see Chapter 3). Since the study was also designed to explore even remotely possible relations involving other principles, further tentative hypotheses were formulated wherever possible (see Chapters 4 to 6).

At the present time, more information is needed about the enduring processes represented by the abilities themselves, and concerning relations between the abilities and other cognitive structures. More than anything else, the correlational results described in Chapters 3 to 6 suggest the value of further consideration of the response *processes* evoked by abilities tests and the place of these processes in a broader scheme of cognitive organization. Clarification of these processes may provide a basis for understanding relations between abilities and other aspects of personality organization.

---

[1] Guilford's (1950) measures of creativity may, however, be related to criterion measures of this principle.

2

METHOD

THE SAMPLE OF SUBJECTS

The present sample comprised sixty-three female college students. Their ages ranged from 17 to 22, the mean being 19.3 years. All subjects were sorority members at a small Midwestern university. Although it was anticipated that the homogeneity of the sample might reduce some of the correlations, this did not appear to be the case, at least for the control-principle measures. For example, the r between the two scores for leveling-sharpening was similar to that observed in previous studies, and the r between scores for Witkin's Embedded Figures and Rod and Frame Tests was considerably *higher* than that reported by Witkin for female college students. In keeping with these observations is the fact that means and sigmas of the control-principle scores were very similar to those observed for earlier samples. Each sorority was paid for the participation of its members in both the individual and group testing sessions.

PROCEDURE

Each subject participated in two batteries of tests: a battery of control-principle tests and related procedures (not all of which are included in the present study) and a battery of ability tests.[1] The control-principle tests were administered to individual subjects within periods of from one week to two months. More important for the present study, the times intervening between com-

[1] The tests of control principles were administered by the first author with Drs. Philip S. Holzman and Richard S. Siegal of The Menninger Foundation. One session of ability testing was conducted by Drs. Gardner and Siegal, the other by Drs. Gardner, Messick, and Jackson.

13

pletion of the control-principle battery and participation in the ability tests varied from one week to nearly six and a half months. Any unreliability of the control-principle measures over time could therefore have reduced predicted correlations between these two groups of tests.

CONTROL PRINCIPLE TESTS

The larger battery of control-principle tests from which those used in the present study were selected was administered to each subject in three sessions: a one-hour session, in groups of three to five subjects, during which the Schematizing Test was administered, and two individual sessions of two hours each. Gough's (1949) Home Index, a measure of socioeconomic status, was also administered in one of these sessions.

Descriptions of the specific procedures used to measure the control principles, together with reviews of other research with these procedures, are presented in detail in Chapters 3, 4, 5, and 6. For convenience, the control principles and the tests and scores used to represent them are listed below.

Field-Articulation

Embedded Figures. Mean log time for solution of the 24 items in Witkin's (1950) modification of Gottschaldt's figures.

Rod and Frame. Average error, total test, for the 24 judgments in all three conditions of Witkin's test.

Constricted-Flexible Control

Color-Word. Color-word interference, represented by a residual score (the difference between reading time for colors printed in incongruous words and the time predicted from the regression of these times on reading times for the colors alone).

Size Estimation. Constant error in judgments of a circular disk bearing a smaller picture.

Leveling-Sharpening

Schematizing. Percentage ranking accuracy and mean percentage increment error in judgments of 150 squares of gradually increasing size.

Equivalence Range

Object Sorting. Number of groups formed in categorizing 73 objects.

Size Constancy (Sensory). The mean diameter of the circular figure judged equal to the standard in "retinal" size.

INTELLECTUAL ABILITY TESTS

The 13 paper-and-pencil tests used to measure the eight intellectual abilities included in the present study were drawn from the *Kit of Selected Tests for Reference Aptitude and Achievement Factors* prepared by committees of experts on factor-analytic studies of abilities, under the editorship of John W. French (1954). The tests were administered to approximately half the subjects in each of two sessions. About two and a half hours were required to administer the battery of tests, plus the Edwards Personal Preference Schedule (Edwards, 1954). Administration of the abilities tests followed the instructions concerning their use that appear in the *Manual* or that are included in the instruction sheets preceding some of the tests. Detailed descriptions of these tests, together with theoretical considerations, are presented in Chapters 3 to 6. The abilities, tests, and scores are listed below.

Flexibility of Closure

Concealed Figures. The number of complex figures correctly marked as containing the simple figure in Thurstone's adaptation of the Gottschaldt figures.

Designs. The number of complex figures correctly marked as containing the simple figure.

Spatial Relations and Orientation

Spatial Orientation. The number of correct identifications of shift in the relation of a boat's prow to the horizon from one picture to another.

Cards. The number of correct identifications of rotated figures that are like the standard figures.

Verbal Knowledge

Wide Range Vocabulary. The number of synonyms correctly identified.

General Reasoning

Mathematics Aptitude. The number of correct answers.

Ideational Fluency

Thing Categories. The number of words produced in two and a half minutes in response to the instruction to "write all the *things that are round or could be called round*."

Associative Memory

Picture-Number. The number of pictures correctly numbered immediately following the learning period.

Word-Number. The number of words correctly numbered immediately following the learning period.

Induction

Letter Grouping. The number of items correctly marked on the basis of the rule induced from the examples.

Marks. The number of items correctly marked on the basis of the rule induced from the examples.

Deduction

False Premises. The number of correct and incorrect conclusions (based on formal syllogisms) correctly identified.

Reasoning. The number of correct conclusions the subject provides based on examples that are formal syllogisms.

ADDITIONAL SCORES

The Edwards Personal Preference Schedule yields scores purportedly representing achievement, deference, order, exhibition, autonomy, affiliation, intraception, succorance, dominance, abasement, nurturance, change, endurance, heterosexuality, and aggression.

Additional scores included the percentage incorrect in response to each associative memory test; the percentage round for the Things Categories Test; level of abstraction scores for the Object Sorting Test; and the socioeconomic status score provided by Gough's Home Index.

ANALYSIS OF THE DATA

The predictions made in the present study lent themselves to the use of a correlational design. Since the hypotheses had direct implications for the clustering of test performances, correlations between the batteries of cognitive control and ability scores could be factor analyzed by Tucker's (1958) interbattery method. This method permits a determination of common sources of variance that is not based on correlations between tests *within* the two batteries.

A principal components factor analysis was also performed with all correlations among 22 key scores (further selection was aided by results of the interbattery analysis). The scores derived from Gough's Home Index and from the fifteen scales of the Edwards Personal Preference Schedule were excluded from this second analysis because results of the interbattery analysis suggested that they were contributing little, if anything, to the understanding of relationships between the two batteries of tests. The additional scores derived from tests representing the *associative memory* ability were also omitted, because of their extremely high correlations with the usual scores for these tests. The level of abstraction scores were used in a subsequent analysis described in Chapter 6 and also were not included in the principal components analysis.

The two factor analyses employed, and the similar results they yielded, are described in detail in Chapter 7.

3

FIELD-ARTICULATION, CONSTRICTED-FLEXIBLE CONTROL, AND THE ABILITIES OF FLEXIBILITY OF CLOSURE AND SPATIAL RELATIONS AND ORIENTATION

Two of the major hypotheses of the study concern the field-articulation control principle and the abilities called flexibility of closure and spatial relations and orientation. Following consideration of the field-articulation principle, and the *constricted-flexible control* principle, which appeared to merge with it in the study by Gardner et al. (1959), the two ability concepts are described. The specific hypotheses concerning relations between field-articulation and these abilities are then presented. In this chapter and in Chapters 4, 5, and 6, considerable emphasis is placed upon the development of rationales for control principles and abilities, and the test responses used to represent them. The full meaning of the hypotheses and the results can be apprehended only in the light of these rationales.

The Field-Articulation Principle

As in the study by Gardner et al. (1959), the term *field-articulation* will be used to refer to a dimension of individual differences in ego functioning originally described by Witkin and his co-

18

workers (1954) in terms of "field dependence-independence."[1] Results of the study by Gardner et al., like the results described by Witkin et al., indicated that the essence of this dimension is not the degree of dependence upon the *external* field. Neither does the dimension seem limited to individual differences in the capacity to extract embedded "items" from their surrounds. A cursory examination of Witkin's Rod and Frame Test might suggest that successful performance implies a general capacity to respond to internal (in this case, gravity) cues, whereas unsuccessful performance implies a general dependence upon external cues. However, the significant correlations repeatedly observed between performances on this test and performances on Witkin's modification of Gottschaldt's (1926, 1929) embedded figures test are among the results which suggest that the individuals actually differ in their capacity to *articulate*, or differentiate, complex stimulus fields. Results of the study by Gardner et al. (1959) indicated that the operation of a field-articulation principle may be particularly evident in instances of "perceived incongruity," that is, when effective performance demands that attention be directed to one of two sets of cues that induce opposing response tendencies. The fact that persons adept at field-articulation could also inhibit response to irrelevant embedded *items* while attending to relevant *surrounds* supported the interpretation of the dimension as representing generalized individual differences in the selectiveness of attention. Further evidence that the articulation of fields, rather than the more limited capacity to "extract items from surrounds," is sampled in these tests can be found in studies by Jackson (1955), Podell and Phillips (1959), and Gardner and Long (in preparation, c), which show that these individual differences are apparent (a) whether the irrelevant stimuli are organized or unorganized and (b) whether the irrelevant stimuli are embedded items or embedding contexts.

Other findings by Gardner et al. suggesting the generality of the structures which determine these individual differences included the facility in free associating characteristic of subjects high in field-articulation. When asked to say everything that came to their

---

[1] Two obvious possibilities are not dealt with in the present study: (a) that opposite extremes of field-articulation and the other cognitive control principles may represent qualitatively different psychical structures; and (b) that more than one type of personality organization may lead to performances representing one extreme of a cognitive control principle.

minds after hearings the stimulus words "Dry" or "House," these subjects' ease and rapidity of associating suggested that they could selectively direct attention to (in psychoanalytic terms, hyper-cathect) elements of memory schemata relevant to these words without being distracted by the multitude of less relevant memories. Under these conditions, the selection of responses seemed much like the selective attention required in embedded figures tests and in other situations in which the subject is confronted with relevant and irrelevant stimuli, and in which the instructions or the nature of the task make it clear which are relevant and which irrelevant to the adaptive intention involved.

In addition to these findings, the field-articulation principle also seemed to guide response to tests of constricted-flexible control, a dimension of ego organization originally employed by Klein (1954) to account for individual differences in cognitive behavior under conditions of thirst. The present study provided an opportunity for a partial further test of this finding.

The fact that subjects know what is required of them in these situations before responding means that the selectiveness with which they attend to relevant stimuli may show itself immediately upon their perceiving the stimulus field. It should be made explicit here, too, that selectiveness of attention may *or may not* involve orient-ing movements of the perceptual apparatus (e.g., eye movements). Simple introspection reveals that one can, without moving the eye, for example, concentrate on a small foveal object, broaden the span of attention to include more peripheral objects, or turn attention inward to a memory so intently that the entire external field is but dimly perceived. In other situations, orienting movements of the eye may serve as the means by which attention is directed. These observations are directly in line with many earlier views of atten-tion, in all of which selectiveness has been explicitly recognized.

The fact that one of the cognitive controls governing attention may be central to these laboratory tests does not, of course, mean that the entire constellation of individual consistencies observed by Witkin and others can be explained in this way. Generalized ten-dencies toward passive, nonanalytical, or active, analytical response may underlie the larger constellation of behaviors involved. In the original study of this dimension of individual consistency, Witkin and his co-workers (1954) showed relationships between responses to a variety of laboratory tests in which differential response to "competing" cues was essential for adequate performance and responses to clinical tests and interviews. The prominent among the clinical findings were indications that "field-dependence" (low field-articulation) is associated with general passivity, poor awareness and poor control of impulses, low self-esteem, and relatively primitive body image. Witkin's findings concerning responses to the Rorschach Test were largely confirmed in the study of *relationships* between cognitive control principles (Gardner et al., 1959).

In addition to the studies of this dimension referred to by Gardner et al. (1959), a study by Scott, Bexton, Heron, and Doane (1959) should be mentioned here. These investigators showed that perceptual isolation has, among other results, dramatic deleterious effects upon performances in various tests. Two of these —the Thurstone-Gottschaldt Test and the Kohs Blocks Test— involve the kind of selective attention required by core laboratory tests of field-articulation. Since it is well known that such isolation produces a gradual increase in hypercathexis of internal stimuli appropriate to primary-process rather than secondary-process thinking, these subjects' performances after isolation can be conceived of as indicating difficulty in redirecting attention to the external world and in achieving normal levels of refinement in the differential hypercathexis of external objects. Like the other findings referred to above, these results can be understood within the framework of cognitive controls governing attention.

Thurstone (1944) and Eysenck, Granger, and Brengelmann (1957) have obtained factors indicating relations between response to embedded figures tests, the Müller-Lyer illusion, and block design tests. The latter factor also included response to the angular illusion of Cymbalistyj. Gardner (in press) recently showed that the field-articulation principle in part determines response to illusions of a certain *type* including a difficult Müller-Lyer figure. Gardner and Long (in preparation, a) have found evidence to support Gollin and Baron's (1954) finding of links between performance on an embedded figures test and performance on a retroactive inhibition test (see Chapter 5).

Among the large body of other researches relevant to this control principle are several studies showing correlates of performance in embedded figures tests (of the general kind providing a core measure of field-articulation). Pemberton's (1952a, 1952b) studies of relations between embedded figures test responses and tempermental aspects of behavior are relevant here, although she discussed these results primarily in terms of the flexibility of closure ability, which is also measured by embedded figures tests. Pemberton commented upon earlier studies showing relations between rapid solution times in embedded figures tests and social detachment (Smith, 1951); interest in physical science (Gehlmann, 1951); and theoretical interest (Jay, 1950). She considered her corroboration of these findings as further evidence of relations to Witkin's results. Pemberton also found these subjects to be interested in "analytical" endeavors, which seems directly related to Witkin's findings.

Podell and Phillips (1959) have shown that this control principle is linked to a dimension of "decontextualization" defined earlier by Phillips and others.

From the standpoint of the generality of these controls, the most intriguing related findings may appear in studies of the "adaptive flexibility" factor by Guilford et al. (e.g., 1957). This factor had loadings on tests called "Match Problems" and related procedures similar to those employed earlier by Duncker (1935), as well as on an embedded figures test. These "insight" tests also can be thought of as requiring selective attention to relevant stimuli or ideas in the face of compelling stimuli or ideas leading to more obvious but less effective attempts at solution. This *flexibility* of selective attention in solving adaptive problems is analogous to the flexibility shown by subjects high in field-articulation in laboratory tests. That is, these subjects seem capable of selectively attending to relevant versus irrelevant cues, memories, or ideas with a flexibility that overrides the particular organizational properties of the "field." These results suggest that subjects who are adept at selective attention under various conditions are able to relinquish dominant sets with relative ease. That is, they are able to direct attention flexibly to nondominant ideas or modes of solution, when such direction is adaptively relevant. An unpublished study by Goodman (cited by Rokeach, 1960) supports this assumption.

The field-articulation principle should also be studied in relation to the work of Cattell (e.g., 1957), who describes a factor of *critical practicality* (U.I. 19) that includes an embedded figures test score. Even more intriguing is the possibility of relations to the second-order factor of *dependent sociability vs. self-sufficiency* (or *group identification vs. individuality*) identified by Cattell. This general factor has a defining loading on critical practicality and seems to include interpersonal attitudes quite similar to those Witkin and others have described as correlates of the dimension of consistency here referred to as field-articulation.

FIELD-ARTICULATION AS SELECTIVENESS OF ATTENTION: THEORETICAL CONSIDERATIONS

Although the findings referred to above indicate that field-articulation is an important aspect of adaptive behavior with implications for several other aspects of personality organization, the response mechanisms that may account for the consistent individual differences observed in the criterion laboratory tests have not been fully detailed. It seems clear that this cognitive variable is particularly evident in laboratory tests which require differential direction of attention to adaptively relevant aspects of complex stimulus fields containing "misleading" cues. It is not clear, however, *how* this cognitive control principle affects laboratory performances.

We have stated that field articulation may have relevance primarily to selectiveness of attention under certain stimulus conditions. Since this cognitive control principle and the other principles have been conceived of within the general framework of psychoanalytic theory, it may be well to consider attention and its direction first from the psychoanalytic point of view. The discussion of the attentional behaviors subsumed under field-articulation will also include consideration of two recent theoretical developments that may bear upon the specific response mechanisms evoked by tests of field-articulation and tests of the intellectual abilities called flexibility of closure and spatial relations and orientation.

This brief discussion of the place of attention in psychoanalytic theory is based in part upon the excellent summaries and schematic outlines of psychoanalytic theory provided by Rapaport (e.g., 1951c, 1960a, b) as well as upon the original works of Freud (e.g., 1895, 1900, 1911, 1925a, 1925b), Hartmann (e.g., 1939, 1950, 1956), Hartmann, Kris, and Loewenstein (1946), Rapaport et al. (1945), and others. Since the phenomena of attention have not received extensive consideration in recent psychoanalytic works this discussion will begin with some of Freud's earliest writings.

Field-Articulation and the Psychoanalytic View of Attention

Although written at a key point during his transition from neurological to metapsychological theorizing, and thus heavily loaded with neurological speculation, Freud's "Project for a Scientific Psychology" (1895) contains the germs of the conception of attention evident in his later work. In developing the biological view that "unpleasure" is the means by which the infant learns to achieve the first level of effective disposition of attention cathexes Freud noted that in states of expectation the budding ego gradually learns to cathect the perception, rather than the memory image of the wished-for object. As he put it (1895, p. 428): "one must direct one's attention to indications of quality (because they belong to perceptions that may lead to satisfaction) and then allow oneself to be led from the indication of quality to the perception which has emerged. In short, the mechanism of attention must owe its origin to a biological rule of this kind, which will regulate the displacement of ego-cathexes." The early development of this basic form of adaptively effective cathexis is an essential aspect of the emerging awareness of the distinction between the "me" and the "not me" and is essential to the flowering of higher-order, reality attuned, secondary-process functioning.

The problem of attention was considered extensively in The Interpretation of Dreams (1900), in which Freud elaborated upon the conception of primary and secondary functions. As he put it

> All that I insist upon is the idea that the activity of the *first* . . system is directed towards securing the *free discharge* of the quantities of excitation, while the *second* system, by means of the cathexes emanating from it, succeeds in *inhibiting* this discharge and in transforming the cathexis into a quiescent one, no doubt with a simultaneous raising of its level. I presume, therefore, that under the dominion of the second system the discharge of excitation is governed by quite different mechanical conditions from those in force under the dominion of the first system. When once the second system has concluded its exploratory thought-activity, it releases the inhibition and damming-up of the excitations and allows them to discharge themselves in movement [1900, pp. 599-600; see also Freud, 1915b].

Freud pointed out that successful adaptation requires that "thinking must aim at freeing itself more and more from exclusive regulation by the unpleasure principle and at restricting the development of affect in thought-activity to the minimum required for acting as a signal" (p. 602). Thus, the energies involved in secondary-process functioning are a relatively neutralized quantity available for channeling and direction in ways determined by the higher levels of cognitive organization. The next major advance in the psychoanalytic conception of attention appeared in 1911 in Freud's "Formulations on the Two Principles of Mental Functioning." There he elaborated still further upon the employment of this neutralized energy in the service of the reality principle as secondary-process functions gradually become more differentiated. As he described it, this energy is employed in continual scanning of the external world (including both pleasant and unpleasant objects), as a means of preparation for action should a need arise.

As use of the reality principle increases in development, ego *structures* emerge that include patterns of distribution of attention cathexis. Even at the early point in his thinking represented by the "Project," Freud referred to the ego as "a *constant* cathexis" (1895, p. 417). The concept of structure, not explicitly developed until much later (see Freud, 1923), is a key aspect of current psychoanalytic theory (see Rapaport, 1951c, 1957, 1960a) and is essential to a psychoanalytic view of more complex aspects of the distribution of attention cathexis that emerge in development subsequent to the initial stage of differentiation between memory images and perceptions described above. In fact, as Rapaport (e.g., 1951c, p. 76) has pointed out, the concept of structure represents a major difference between the psychoanalytic theory and other current theories. In this conception, "structure" refers to relatively enduring organizations of processes. Rapaport (1957) has described these structural organizations as "tools of cognition."

It should be noted here that recent developments in psychoanalytic theory (see Hartmann, 1939; Rapaport, 1960a, b) point to an additional possibility—that the autonomous apparatuses involved in ego functioning are (a) the source, or (b) a contributory source of attention cathexis.

The defense mechanisms (see Anna Freud, 1936) are foremost among the structures that have direct implications for the distribution of attention cathexis. The concept of defense is based upon the postulation that, in the course of development, some of the energy represented by drives is employed in enduring counter-cathectic operations that rechannel the expression of drives. Individual variations in ego formation, including the defensive functions, are considered products of (a) the constitutionally given characteristics of the apparatuses (e.g., memoric, perceptual) employed by the ego (see, for example, Freud, 1937, p. 337; Hartmann, 1939; Holzman and Gardner, 1959) and (b) the individual's experience, including the influence of the persons providing the context for the emerging pattern of person and object relations. The specifically directed energies used in defensive functioning are not available to the ego for hypercathexis of either ideas or perceptions. In line with this conception, it is a clinical commonplace that persons involved in unusually severe drive-defense struggles show limitations in the amount of energy available for spontaneous attention and for concentration. The amount of expendable energy available to the individual is in part a function of the adequacy of synthesis (see Nunberg, 1931; Freud, 1937, p. 337) of drives and reality constraints that the ego represents.

Using a small part of the "neutral" and/or "neutralized" energies available to it, the ego "periodically sends out small amounts of cathectic energy into the perceptual system and by their means samples the external stimuli, and after every such groping advance draws back again" (Freud, 1925b, p. 185). A similar point of view is expressed in "A Note Upon the 'Mystic Writing-Pad'" (Freud, 1925a). Freud believed that when attention cathexis is so recruited to ongoing activity in the perceptual apparatus (or to accessible ideas or memories), consciousness is attained. Thus an intimate relation exists between the distribution of attention cathexis and the nature of consciousness itself.[2]

Rapaport has suggested that "different degrees of hypercathecting combined with countercathecting are at work in and determine the character of selective apperception" (1951a, p. 714). Although he made this statement in discussing the cathexis of ideas in the course of thinking, it is also relevant to the channeling of attention

[2] Klein (1959) has recently dealt with the problem of consciousness in psychoanalytic theory in considerable detail, including reference to certain control principles.

to the perceptual system. He pointed out there and in his discussion, with Gill and Schafer (1945), of the Digit Span and Arithmetic subtests of the Wechsler-Bellevue, that attention, conceived of as effortless cathexis, shades gradually into concentration as the situation requires more and more directed, selective focusing of attention. As Rapaport has pointed out (1951a, p. 716), when the person is concentrating, it is as if a "quasi-need [see Lewin, 1935] has been created which gathers the still available attention-cathexes —and perhaps also available, not fully neutralized, cathexes corresponding to ego-interests."

This sketch of a few major points in the psychoanalytic conception of attention provides us with a view of (a) the origins of directed attention in the biological facts of adaptation; (b) the general place of attention in reality-oriented behavior; (c) structures governing the availability of directable energies after the earliest phases of development; and (d) general implications of the defense concept for attention. Although each of the defenses has unique implications for certain aspects of attention (see, for example, Freud's [1926] discussion of the defense of isolation and certain aspects of concentration), the structures determining the selectiveness of attention subsumed under field-articulation may not represent the generalization of defensive operations to relatively neutral situations. It is just as likely (see Holzman and Gardner, 1959) that certain general principles of cognitive organization (i.e., control principles) serve as preconditions for defenses.

Thus, the definition of field-articulation offered by Gardner et al. (1959) implies the existence of enduring organizations of the cognitive processes involved in the selective disposition of neutralized cathectic energies in the face of compelling stimulation, ideas, memory schemata, "sets," etc., that are irrelevant and misleading in terms of the adaptive requirement the person is trying to fulfill. The field-articulation principle represents a dimension of individual differences in selectiveness (and, presumably, the structures determining selectiveness). The principle thus refers to one important facet of secondary-process functioning that is relevant to a broad class of situations, although not relevant to other classes. It can be thought of as representing the refinement and differentiation of structures relevant to one aspect of effective concentration. As such, it could be linked to the defense of isolation, which Freud (1926) in part defined in terms of the capacity to concentrate. Although ratings of isolation in terms of "obsessiveness" in response to the Rorschach were not significantly related to field-articulation in the study by Gardner et al. (1959), isolation is also presumed to be involved in compulsive behavior—with or without obsessive elaborations—so that links between this control principle and the defense of isolation may be revealed in further studies.

In some ways, this view of the field-articulation principle is similar to Schachtel's (e.g., 1959) recent emphasis on the adaptive importance of "focal" attention. Studies of cognitive controls have suggested, however, that several relatively independent control principles determine different aspects of attention, and that no one control is dominant in all situations.

If the *amount* of energy available for hypercathexis of perceptions of external objects were the key variable accounting for individual differences in field-articulation tests, one might predict performances on the Embedded Figures Test if he had information concerning the intensity of the person's dynamic struggles, or the degree of synthesis of drives and reality constraints he has achieved. It seems unlikely, however, that "ego strength" will be highly correlated with performances in field-articulation tests. The most extreme field-articulator among over three hundred persons tested with these procedures in The Menninger Foundation's laboratories suffered from a severe, long-standing personality disorder, in part manifested by self-imposed social isolation and overideational symptoms, and was apparently employing his adroitness in field-articulation in the service of extreme projection.

Since psychoanalytic theory may not include *specific* mechanism-constructs that would account for field-articulating behaviors, we shall consider two current theories of attentional behavior that are not incompatible with the general theoretical framework described above and that may offer some insight into the particular behaviors involved in field-articulation.

Field-Articulation in Relation to Piaget's Studies of Attention

In a series of *Recherches* reported in the *Archives de Psychologie* from 1942 to 1956, Piaget and his co-workers have offered intriguing, and in some instances impressive, evidence that *strategies of attending,* rather than perception per se, are linked to sensorimotor intelligence, and through it to more general schemata of cognitive organization (see, for example, Piaget, 1947). According to Piaget, perception is a relatively low-order aspect of human functioning and involves certain built-in distortions that are overcome only by the gradual development of effective strategies of attending. In visual functioning, for example, an innate tendency to overestimate the sizes of objects in the center of the attentional field is, according to Piaget, gradually compensated for in the course of development by progressive "decentration." By means of effective decentration (in visual perception usually, but not necessarily, in the form of eye movements), the adult overcomes the distortions inherent in the operation of the perceptual apparatus and succeeds in coordinating himself to the external world. Fraisse, Ehrlich, and Vurpillot (1956) have provided evidence that when there is a discrepancy between attention and regard, the former takes precedence. That is, centration effects result from attentional centering, rather than simply from visual fixations.

Piaget's description of the development of perceptual activity (see, for example, Piaget, 1947) is in many ways similar to Witkin's description of the development of field-independence. Like Witkin, Piaget has used the term "global" to describe the perceptual behavior of children and the term "analytical" to describe the perceptual behavior of older children and adults. Gardner (in press) has shown that two principles—field-articulation and scanning—differentially affect subjects' ability to overcome two types of illusions. Gardner and Long (1960a, b) have confirmed key findings reported in the *Recherches*. Gardner (1959; in press) and Gardner and Long (in preparation, b, c) have shown that an independent scanning control principle governs the extensiveness with which attention is directed in free scanning. These findings with adults suggest that the general progression during development from global to active, analytical dispositions of attention that Piaget has described may be divisible into at least two sets of cognitive controls. Although Piaget has not considered such functions as those involved in the Rod and Frame Test in detail, his general conception of attention can be applied to the direction of attention to bodily cues in the face of misleading visual cues as well as to the direction of attention to particular cues in a complex of cues presented in one perceptual modality. Piaget and von Albertini

(1950) have shown developmental improvement in the capacity to overcome the Müller-Lyer illusion, and Gardner (in press) has shown that this capacity in adults involves the field-articulation principle. It seems possible, therefore, that Piaget's developmental findings are directly related to Witkin's (1959) findings concerning the development of field-articulation.

Piaget's emphasis upon attentional schemata as essential components of effective adaptation is in some ways similar to Rapaport's (1953) discussion of the progression from passivity to activity in the course of ego development. Both authors also conceive of perception as but one aspect of cognition. Perceptual development is seen as intimately linked to the progessive emergence of more general cognitive structures. Piaget's systematic study of the perceptions of children has led him "to introduce a distinction between instantaneous perceptions which are always passive and a 'perceptual activity' connecting them with each other in space and time, according to certain remarkable laws (in particular a mobility and reversibility increasing with age)" (1936, p. xi). His conception of attentional strategies also has much in common with Hebb's (e.g., 1949, pp. 4-5) emphasis upon the active, spontaneous selectiveness involved in attention.

A Gestalt-Psychological View of Perceptual Articulation

Köhler and Adams (1958) have shown that the *differentiation* with which a stimulus complex is experienced is a function of the intensity or unequivocality with which attention is directed to it. To account for this fact, they have offered the conception that the visual cortex is an open system. As they put it, visual attention has the effect of recruiting energy from other parts of the brain to the visual cortex, with the result that processes in the visual cortex are intensified and become more differentiated:

> Quite apart from the energy inherent in afferent impulses, the visual cortex may, or may not, receive energy from other parts of the brain. The former condition seems to be realized when a person takes interest in his visual field. For, under these circumstances, the segregation of objects in the field is sharpened, differences between various parts of the field are enhanced, and so forth [p. 497].

Köhler and Adams have also pointed out that the entire visual field is not necessarily involved: "What we call 'visual attention' may be directed toward particular parts of the visual scene" (p. 498).

In the light of this formulation, it may be that the extreme field-articulator immediately experiences the stimulus complexes confronting him in the Embedded Figures Test, Rod and Frame Test, and related situations as highly differentiated by virtue of the intensity and unequivocality with which he directs attention to the task at hand. It is difficult to see, however, how this formulation would apply to difficult items in the Embedded Figures Test, in which the figure to be extracted is so well camouflaged that perceptual "recognition" is all but impossible. Most subjects who find these simple figures do so by "tracing" them with eye movements. It is also difficult to see how the Köhler and Adams conception of attention would account for performances in the Rod and Frame Test, which requires differential response to *gravity* cues in the face of misleading *visual* cues.

Although Piaget's conception of attention and its place in cognitive behavior was developed in antithesis to the Gestalt point of view, it seems possible that the "perceptual activity" he describes is more compatible with Köhler's satiation theory and attention theory than has previously been stated. It is not inconceivable, for example, that as attention is focused upon successive portions of a complex field, the intensity of the energy recruited to the visual cortex determines the degree of articulation characterizing individual "fixations." In both cases (see Köhler and Adams, 1958, on attention as a determinant of satiation effects), attention is the major variable and takes precedence over the *mechanisms* by which it is presumed to have its effects upon perception. It is also possible that the amount of free energy available to a person and his skill in perceptual activity may be correlated phenomena.

Summary of the View of Field-Articulation Guiding This Study

Although experiments are needed to delineate the ways in which field-articulation manifests itself in perceptual behavior, the psychoanalytic view of relations between attention and perception, which is generally compatible with Piaget's approach, seems to provide a framework in which to conceptualize schemata guiding the direction of attention. In the present study, field-articulation was conceived of primarily as a principle of cognitive organization apparent in the selectiveness of attention under certain circumstances, rather than the quality or intensity of attention once directed. Thus, individual differences in articulating stimuli in the Embedded Figures Test are presumed to be closely linked to the efficiency with which the subject "surveys" the complex figures. It must be noted, however, that two subjects could be similar in modes of sampling complex fields but different in the experienced articulation of the segment viewed at any instant. Or, both perceptual activity and immediate perceptual articulation may improve in the course of development, so that they operate together to make the adult more effective than the child—and the high field-articulator more effective than the low field-articulator—in certain adaptive situations.

FIELD-ARTICULATION AND CONSTRICTED-FLEXIBLE CONTROL

In the study of relationships between cognitive control principles (Gardner et al., 1959), the field-articulation principle seemed to merge with the constricted-flexible control principle originally used by Klein (1954) to account for the effects of thirst on cognitive behavior. Although the core size estimation test was deliberately altered for the larger study the present subjects participated in, the Color-Word Test seemed to provide an adequate measure of constricted-flexible control.

THE FLEXIBILITY OF CLOSURE ABILITY

This ability factor has appeared frequently in earlier studies. Criterion tests include Thurstone's modification of Gottschaldt's embedded figures test and similar procedures. Since this factor is apparent in response to embedded figures tests—one of several types of situations in which the operation of a field-articulation principle has been evident—it has obvious relations to the more broadly conceived cognitive variable originally described by Witkin et al.

French describes the factor as: "The ability to keep in mind a definite configuration so as to identify it in spite of perceptual distractions" (1954, p. 6). This interpretation emphasizes the often-overlooked memory aspect of the criterion tests (see Gardner et al.,

1959, Ch. 8), but does not include an attempt to specify the means by which the complex designs are articulated. As indicated in the sections below on the rationales of key tests of this ability, selective attention may be crucial to successful performance in embedded figures tests. It seems unlikely that the phenomena of "closure" are relevant here even if individual differences in extraction times reflect the articulation of immediate experience.

THE SPATIAL RELATIONS AND ORIENTATION ABILITY

Abilities relevant to the solution of adaptive problems involving space, spatial relations, visualization of rotations in space, etc., have been explored in a great many studies. Thurstone (1950) and Air Force psychologists (see Guilford, 1947) spoke of three major spatial abilities that are distinct but correlated. In the "Kit" of reference tests (French, 1954), these were reduced to two: spatial relations and orientation, and visualization. The second of these had to be omitted from the present study because of limitations on our subjects' time. Fruchter (1954), Michael (1954), and Michael, Guilford, Fruchter, and Zimmerman (1957) are among those who have commented upon the difficulties encountered in attempts to clarify the number of abilities in this area. Zimmerman (1954a, b) has suggested that some of these problems may result from differences in the difficulty of various spatial tests and has postulated that tests in this general area may be responded to with processes ranging from perceptual speed, at the simple level, to reasoning, at the most difficult level. He has also pointed out that individuals may solve spatial problems at particular levels of difficulty by different methods, thus further obscuring relationships between spatial abilities.

Barratt (1953) and Tomkins (1951) have collected introspective reports concerning subjects' modes of solution of the spatial problems presented in ability tests. Both sets of results indicate that differences in scores are associated with variations in modes of solution. These results will be considered in the sections on the rationales of these tests.

Fruchter (1954) has summarized a number of studies showing the general superiority of males over females in spatial tests. Barratt (1955) has provided further evidence supporting these earlier findings. Since these differences parallel those commonly observed in tests of field-articulation, they seem to support the hypothesis of relations between this control principle and spatial abilities. Developmental curves for spatial abilities may also be roughly similar to those of field-articulation (see Fruchter, 1954; Witkin, 1959). Barratt (1955) has provided another finding that points to a link between field-articulation and spatial abilities. One of the spatial factors in his studies included a defining loading on the spatial orientation test used in the present study. Responses of high-scoring subjects to Thurstone's Temperament Schedule were interpreted as indicating ability to concentrate in the face of distractions. This was the only temperament variable related to spatial factors in that study and seems directly in line with the conception that the field-articulation control involves selective attention in the face of distractions and may be linked to spatial abilities.

Barratt's (1955) finding that his female subjects showed a general spatial ability factor, whereas his male subjects showed greater differentiation of spatial abilities, is discussed in Chapter 8 in connection with results of the present study.

The definition of the spatial relations and orientation ability by French is as follows: "The ability to comprehend the nature of the arrangement of elements within a visual stimulus pattern primarily with reference to the location of the examinee" (1954, p. 23). This definition in itself suggests that field-articulation, as defined earlier in this chapter, plays an important part in the response processes involved in tests of the ability. The first part of the definition, concerning "comprehend the nature of the arrangement of elements," seems to imply the sort of selective attention required in Witkin's Embedded Figures Test. This reinterpretation of some of the processes involved in response to these ability tests will be elaborated upon in the sections concerning their rationales included in this chapter.

HYPOTHESES

Significant correlations were predicted between the following:

1.   Scores for field-articulation (CC 1, CC 2) and constricted-flexible control (CC 3, CC 4).

2.   Scores for field-articulation and flexibility of closure (A 1, A 2).

3. Scores for field-articulation and spatial relations and orientation (A 3, A 4).

The second hypothesis is based on the obvious similarity between Witkin's Embedded Figures Test and flexibility of closure tests. Hypothesis 2 could also be arrived at from some of Thurstone's (1944) results, from results of some of the studies summarized by French (1951), and recent studies by Rudin and Stagner (1958), Crutchfield et al. (1958), and Podell and Phillips (1959).

In respect to the third hypothesis, some of the studies summarized by French (1951), e.g., those reported by Guilford (1947), and the study by Podell and Phillips (1959) suggest substantial correlations between "extraction" tests and spatial tests. In addition, Eysenck et al. (1957, p. 121) describe a factor including performances in the Gottschaldt, Block Designs, and "Primary Mental Ability" space tests.

TESTS AND MEASURES OF FIELD-ARTICULATION

EMBEDDED FIGURES TEST

Apparatus and Procedure

Witkin (1950) increased the difficulty of Gottschaldt's (1926) items by adding colors to all but one of the complex figures used. The subject must "find" one of eight simple figures in each of twenty-four complex figures. A complex figure is shown for 15 seconds, then a simple figure is shown for 10 seconds. The simple figure is removed, and the complex figure presented again. The simple and complex figures are not shown simultaneously. In the present study, the subject was instructed to tell the experimenter as soon as she discovered the simple figure, then to trace it with a stylus. If the subject requested it, she was allowed to see the figure again while searching for it.

Rationale

This test was used by Witkin et al. (1954) and has been used frequently in subsequent studies of the individual consistencies he described. It was also used in the study by Gardner et al. (1959) of relationships between cognitive control principles. The high field-articulation factor loadings for solution times with both the easy and difficult items of this test in that study suggested that they are among the most adequate measures of field-articulation.

Earlier results summarized by Gardner et al. (1959) suggested that some part in determining solution times may be played by the leveling-sharpening principle (see Chapter 5), which deals with the formation and preservation of memories (in this case, memories of the simple figures). The ability to attend selectively to relevant segments of the complex figures is much more important, however, in determining solution times in this test.

The requirement to extract simple from complex figures in this test falls into the class of phenomena Hebb (1949, p. 21) has spoken of as "nonsensory" figure-ground organizations, in that "the boundaries of the figure are not fixed by gradients of luminosity in the visual field." Thus, simple articulation of the complex stimuli at the perceptual level (e.g., along the lines used by Gestalt psychologists to account for sensory figure-ground phenomena) is not sufficient for rapid performance. Under the guidance of an adequate memory image of the simple figure, which must be maintained during the period of search in this test, the subject must scan the complex figure effectively. To perform optimally, he must consider only the subunits of the complex figure that are of roughly the same size and shape as the simple figure. Any deviation from the standard set by the simple figure can lead to errors of identification (a common occurrence among slow performers), with consequent extension of correct solution time.

In some of the easiest items, the simple figure can be "recognized" more or less immediately in the complex figure. In some of the more difficult items the simple figure must be "traced" by means of eye movements. In a few of the items it is all but impossible to experience the simple figures as *Gestalten* when they are presented in the complex figures: they must be isolated from the remainder of the complex figures by a kind of visual tracing and often cannot be experienced as complete entities even after they have been identified. Thus, the Embedded Figures Test is similar to the Rod and Frame Test in requiring selective attention to parts of complex stimulus fields in such a way as to overcome the effects of distracting cues.

Score

CC 1. *Mean log time.* The score consisted of the mean log solution time for the twenty-four items. The odd-even reliability coefficient (corrected by the Spearman-Brown formula) was .95 in the present study.

ROD AND FRAME TEST

Apparatus and Procedure

This test is described in detail in the original book on field-dependence and field-independence (Witkin et al., 1954). The apparatus consists of a luminous rod within a luminous frame, and a chair from which the subject can view the frame and the rod with body erect, or with body tilted 28 degrees to the left or the right. The subject sits seven feet in front of the luminous rod-and-frame apparatus in a room that is otherwise totally dark. The subject is required to direct the experimenter to adjust the rod so that it is "straight with the walls" of the room. In the first eight trials, the chair is tilted 28 degrees to the left; in the second eight, 28 degrees to the right; and in the last eight, the chair is upright. In half of the trials in the first two conditions, the body and frame are tilted in the same direction; in the other half, they are tilted in the opposite direction.

Rationale

In the study by Gardner et al. (1959), scores for the Rod and Frame Test had strong loadings on the field-articulation factor for female subjects. This finding is in keeping with Witkin's results but indicates a stronger relation to performance in the Embedded Figures Test than he reported.

As in the Embedded Figures Test, effective performance requires selective direction of attention to certain cues in the field and inattention to other cues that are compelling but irrelevant. The frame is in all cases misleading; attention must be directed to the gravity cues. This cross-modality problem in selective attention obviously involves many response attributes that are not involved in the Embedded Figures Test. It is not surprising, for example, that the "competition" between visual and gravity cues in the Rod and Frame Test introduces numerous sources of variance unrelated to field-articulation. What is impressive is that in Witkin's study, as in the studies by Gardner et al. and other investigators, an essential similarity between the response processes involved in these two tests is revealed in highly significant correlations and corresponding factor loadings.

Score

CC 2. *Average error, total test.* In the present study, the average-error value for the entire test was employed. In earlier studies, scores for the three major parts of the test were used, in addition to a total score. There are indications that the body-erect condition may provide the best measure of field-articulation, but correlations between the three parts of the test have been sufficiently high in previous studies to allow use here of the more stable score representing the entire test. In the present study, the corrected odd-even reliability coefficient for this measure was .92.

TESTS AND MEASURES OF CONSTRICTED-FLEXIBLE CONTROL

COLOR-WORD TEST

Apparatus and Procedure

In Thurstone's (1944) adaptation of Stroop's (1935) test, subjects are required to name (a) the words on a "warm-up" page consisting of four color names (red, green, yellow, blue) typed in black and presented in random order in ten lines containing ten words each; (b) the colors on a page consisting of the four color strips corresponding to the color names; (c) the colors on a page consisting of the four color names each printed in a different one of the four colors (for example, the word "red" may be printed in the color blue). In each part of the test, the subject is encouraged to read "as fast and as accurately as possible."

Rationale

In the report by Gardner et al. (1959), an attempt was made to detail rationales for various aspects of performance in the three parts of this test. In view of the fact that only the "interference" score is used in the present study, attention will be directed here to aspects of the test that seem to bear upon this measure.

At first glance, this test seems to involve the same adaptive requirements as Witkin's tests of field-articulation. That is, the subject is presented with two conflicting sets of cues, and effective performance requires that he direct his attention to only one of these sets. In the Color-Word Test, however, the overlearned tendency to respond with the *word,* rather than the color name, is extremely compelling. For this reason, the capacity to *inhibit* the irrelevant motoric response is a prime determinant of the "interference" effect. The emphasis placed here on inhibition capacity as a determinant of interference in this test is supported by Spivack, Levine, and Sprigel's (1959) finding that interference is related to inhibition of response in time estimation tests.

The fact that the distracting stimuli are words also introduces response determinants into this test that are not present in field-articulation tests. Foremost among these may be individual differences in the prior formation of memory schemata for words, and the availability of these words to consciousness. The highly "verbal" person, who uses words freely and with facility, may have more difficulty in inhibiting word responses than a person more likely to express himself in action (e.g., the alcoholic, whom Witkin et al. [1959] have found to be relatively field-dependent). Given a sample of subjects who vary randomly, with respect to field-articulation, in the availability of words to consciousness, Color-Word performances may appear to be related to other evidences of field-articulation. Given a sample in which field-articulation and the availability of words to consciousness are positively associated, the relationship may fail to appear. It is unfortunate that the Free Association Test used by Gardner et al. (1959) was not administered to the present subjects, for it might have provided measures of controls other than field-articulation (e.g., scanning, tolerance for unrealistic experiences) that help to determine word availability. Such measures could have been employed (e.g., in the factor analyses, or covariance analysis) to hold these determinants of word availability constant. Vocabulary acquisition alone cannot be considered an adequate control for word availability.

As noted by Gardner et al. (1959), the Color-Word Test is different in another crucial way from the other tests ordinarily employed to measure field-articulation: it contains a physical obstacle to separation of the cues. Response to the irrelevant cues cannot be avoided simply by directing attention to certain parts of the stimulus field. This test is also more difficult than other tests which may involve field-articulation. The unusual difficulty may account for the frequent observations of restlessness and bodily tension during this test, and may make susceptibility to anxiety under such conditions another important extraneous variable.

As was suggested in the preceding study, an important feature of the test may be that successful performance requires the subject to shift readily from one color-word combination to another. Any tendency to "cling" to the solution of an immediately preceding combination seems to make the task much more difficult. Smith and Klein (1953) found that subjects characterized by extreme interference effects were relatively unable to discard search sets developed for a particular kind of Gottschaldt figure when confronted with a second kind requiring a new approach.

Smith and Nyman (1959) have suggested that total time scores may not yield adequate measures of interference, since subjects with similar total scores may be characterized by very different strategies of adaptation within the test.

Score

CC 3. *Interference score.* The score used in the present study is identical to the interference score used by Klein (1954) and Gardner et al. (1959). Each subject's interference score was computed as the difference between his actual reading time on Part III and his predicted time based on the regression of reading time, Part III, on reading time, Part II, for the entire group of subjects. As in the preceding study, reading errors were infrequent, but were penalized in both scores: reading time per unit was multiplied by the number of errors and this value added to the number of seconds required to read the page. The use of a residual score rather than a difference score to gain the best possible estimate of interference effects in this test was based upon the general type of rationale for such scores developed by Lacey (1956) and by Lord (1956). In the present study, the correlation between reading time for Part II and reading time for Part III, on which the residual scores were based, was .65, $p < .001$.

SIZE ESTIMATION TEST

Apparatus and Procedure

The apparatus used to produce the variable circle of light was identical to the one described by Gardner et al. (1959). In the present study, however, all the disks were of the same size (40 mm.); the 7x7-inch backgrounds were flesh-colored, rather than gray; and only one of the three disks used contained a smaller picture on its surface. The subject was required to judge the sizes of three disks—gray, black, and flesh-colored with a smaller picture of a glass on its face—four times each, in ADDA order. The subject was required to adjust the circle of light until it was "exactly the same size" as the disk on the wall at her left. She was allowed to look back and forth as many times as she pleased and to turn the crank controlling the size of the circle of light until she was completely satisfied with her setting.

Rationale

In the original study of constricted-flexible control, Klein, (1954) employed judgments of the sizes of disks bearing pictures as a key measure. Part of this test (referred to as Size Estimation Test II) was replicated in the study by Gardner et al. (1959). In an attempt to delineate more clearly some of the crucial differences between this test and the size estimation test used to represent the scanning control principle, some of the conditions of the original test were changed in the larger study which included the present study. Although it seemed likely that these alterations changed the constant-error score to one representing the scanning principle, rather than the constricted-flexible control principle, it was included for want of the standard score.

In the studies by Gardner et al. (1959) and Gardner (1959; in press), constant error in judging plain circular disks was associated with other performances apparently determined by the scanning control principle. Constant error in judging disks bearing smaller pictures produced very different effects. The pictures produced the illusion (possibly related to that of Delboeuf) that the latter disks were smaller than they would have appeared without the pictures. Under these conditions, constant error was associated with the field-articulation principle, rather than the scanning principle. These results seemed to indicate that subjects high in field-articulation can direct attention selectively *either* to an embedded stimulus, when it is relevant, or to the surround, when it is relevant to the adaptive requirement set up by the instructions.

In the present test, the single disk containing a small figure (a picture of an "old-fashioned" drink, similar to one of the pictures on the disks of the preceding studies with this test) was judged *last* by all subjects. In view of this, and the fact that all of the disks were the same size, the distribution of individual differences was different from that obtained in the preceding study. The presence of the picture on the *last* disk in the present study did not lead to the illusion produced by the presence of pictures on *all* the disks in the preceding study. (The r between constant errors with the disk bearing the glass and the other two disks was .77, $p < .001$, much higher than the correlation between plain and figured disks in the preceding study, in which subjects judged the two types of disks in separate tests involving disks of different sizes.)

Score

CC 4. *Constant error, figured disk.* In spite of the fact that the order of presentation of disks may have determined performances on the final, figured disk, constant error on this disk alone was used as a *possible* score for constricted-flexible control in the present study. The corrected reliability coefficient in the present study was .96.

TESTS AND MEASURES OF FLEXIBILITY OF CLOSURE

CONCEALED FIGURES TEST

Materials and Procedure

This test is Thurstone's adaptation of Gottschaldt's embedded figures test. The subject is required to "find" simple geometric figures in more complex figures. In contrast to Witkin's Embedded Figures Test, color is not used and the subject can look back and forth from the simple to the complex figures at will. The test consists of forty-nine items. The subject is allowed ten minutes in which to find as many as possible of the simple figures in the more complex figures.

Rationale

Except for the memory element in Witkin's Embedded Figures Test, and the lack of colors in the Concealed Figures Test, these procedures—both derived from Gottschaldt's test—are very similar. Like Witkin's test, the Concealed Figures Test seems to involve the ability to direct attention efficiently to parts of the complex figures in such a way as to achieve quick identification of the simple figures. From the point of view of the field-articulation principle, the test seems to provide another opportunity for the individual consistencies apparent in Witkin's wide variety of procedures to manifest themselves.

French's interpretation of the flexibility of closure factor (1954, p. 6), and hence of the tests used to represent it, places more emphasis upon the memorial aspect of response to this test. The "ability to keep in mind a definite configuration" (French, 1954, p. 6) may, however, be less important to rapid identification of the simple figures than facility in selective attention during examination of the complex figure.

Score

A 1. *Number correct.* The score for this test is the number of simple figures correctly identified within the ten-minute time limit.

DESIGNS TEST

Materials and Procedure

The second test used to represent the flexibility of closure factor was also developed by Thurstone. Three hundred complex designs are presented in rows of ten. The subject is required to mark the designs in which a capital Greek letter sigma appears. The sigma figure appears at the top of each page of the test. This test is different from Witkin's Embedded Figures Test or the Concealed Figures Test described above in that the same simple figure is to be discovered in all of the complex figures. As in the Concealed Figures Test, color is not employed. The time limit is two minutes.

Rationale

Finding the simple sigma figure in the more complex designs seems to require (a) a clear image of the simple figure, which is easier to achieve and maintain in this test than in the other two embedded-figures tests, and (b) effective scanning of the complex figures. In contrast to Witkin's Embedded Figures Test, in which simple figures in some of the easy items can be "perceptually recognized" more or less immediately, the complexity and multiplicity of forms in which the simple figure must be discovered in the present test apparently mean that most subjects must visually "trace" the simple figure to identify it in most of the items.

Score

A 2. *Number correct.* The score for this test is the number of items correctly marked within the two-minute time limit.

TESTS AND MEASURES OF SPATIAL RELATIONS AND ORIENTATION

SPATIAL ORIENTATION TEST

Materials and Procedure

This test is Part V of the Guilford-Zimmerman Aptitude Survey. Each of the sixty-seven items confronts the subject with two pictures of water and land scenery seen as if the subject were looking over the prow of a motorboat which changes its position from the first picture to the second. The task is to select, from five accompanying dot-and-dash pairings, the one in which the dot accurately represents the first position of the prow and the dash the new position. The changes referred to by French (1954, p. 25) are "any combination of vertical or horizontal movement and tilt."

Rationale

Optimal performance on this test requires that the subject direct his attention in a rather severely restricted fashion to the prow of the motorboat and certain key lines in the pictures, particularly the horizon. The presence of trees, lines representing waves, etc., in the pictures provides the first source of distracting stimuli. The second source of distraction which the subject must ignore—and which makes this an unusually difficult test—is the changed relationships of the pictures and the frames from the first pictures to the second. This test is thus much more similar to Witkin's Embedded Figures Test and the Concealed Figures Test than might at first appear. Because of the complexity of the relevant and irrelevant cues (the relevant cues also include the subject's bodily position), this is a difficult test that seems to combine features of both Witkin's Embedded Figures and Rod and Frame Tests. From the point of view of the principles of ego organization that may govern response in this test, field-articulation, in the sense of the capacity to direct attention selectively, may be directly relevant. It is important to note that this interpretation assumes that "spatial relations and orientation" is a relatively secondary feature of response to this test.

This interpretation of the major response process involved in the Spatial Orientation Test is not without experimental support. Barratt (1953) and Zimmerman (1954a, b) noted that shifts in the *relationship* between parts in various spatial tests affect the difficulty of such tests. Barratt (1953), who obtained introspective accounts from subjects after this test, anticipated that the Spatial Orientation Test would appear in a space factor largely determined by the subject's capacity to reorient *himself* in relation to the changed relations between the stimuli from first to second pictures. The test actually clustered, however, with tests involving changed relations among parts of figures. His subjects' reports indicated that a majority of them solved these problems without projecting themselves into the problem (high field-articulators?), although some subjects (low field-articulators?) did attempt to achieve solutions by imagining themselves in the pictures. These results also support the assumption that kinesthetic factors are less important in this test than has often been assumed.

Tomkins (1951) also inquired into modes of solution. He reported that subjects with high scores on this test recognized the similarity of the items and adopted a general mode of solution, whereas subjects with low scores tended to approach each problem as a separate entity. He also found that subjects with high $M\%$ scores for the Rorschach Test had high scores on the Spatial Orientation Test. This finding is similar to those of Witkin et al. (1954) and Gardner et al. (1959) concerning relations between Rorschach scores and laboratory test scores.

Score

A 3. *Number correct*. The score for this test is the number correct within the ten-minute time limit.

CARDS TEST

Materials and Procedure

This test was originally developed by Thurstone. Each of the twenty items contains a drawing of a card cut in a particular shape. Some of the cards appear to have holes punched in them. Six other drawings—identical or similar to the original—appear to the right of each of these cards. Some of these drawings are front views. In others, the back side is shown. In either case, these cards may be in rotational positions (90, 180, or 270 degrees) different from that of the original card. In each item, the subject is required to indicate which of the test figures are like the original. Six minutes are allowed for identification of the correct figures.

Rationale

The primary determinants of performance in this test seem to be one form of field-articulation and certain additional response processes that are not elicited by either the Spatial Orientation Test or Witkin's tests. The latter set of processes may appear in response to the requirement to conceive of the stimulus figures in various positions. It seems likely, however, that field-articulation is involved. That is, effective performance requires selective attention, not to the entire figures, but to essential portions, e.g., the corner or corners containing the punched holes, the parts of the figure containing irregularities of shape, etc. The subject who can attend to crucial aspects of the stimulus figure is a significant step ahead of the subject who views the stimuli in a relatively unselective manner. Once attention has been restricted to the crucial aspects of the stimulus figure, the problem of identifying this figure among the six other figures presented in each item becomes much simpler.

Thurstone (1950), Guilford (1947), Barratt (1953), and others have pointed out that a separate spatial factor may be represented in responses to tests involving mental "rotations" of figures. It seems likely that this aspect of the test invokes other response processes than those subsumed under the field-articulation principle.

Score

A 4. *Number correct*. The score is the number of correct identifications within the six-minute time limit.

RESULTS

The significant correlation between the Embedded Figures and Rod and Frame Test scores (Table 1), like that observed by Gardner et al. (1959), is higher than the correlation Witkin et al. (1954) found for female subjects. This result indicates again that individuals show consistent differences in the capacity to direct attention selectively when confronted with cues that tend to induce competing response tendencies, whether the cues are presented in one modality or whether the adaptive problem requires response to cues from one modality and active inattention to certain cues from another modality.

Hypothesis 1, which was based upon the earlier observation of a relationship between measures of field-articulation and constricted-flexible control, is not confirmed. As noted above, the Size Estimation Test was altered in the present study in ways that may make it inadequate for measuring constricted-flexible control. The low correlations with scores from Witkin's tests suggests that the presence of pictures on all disks used in preceding studies of constricted-flexible control may have been the aspect of this test that produced the observed relationship between constant error and field-articulation scores. The Color-Word Test, however, was identical to that used in both preceding studies of constricted-flexible control. As noted in the section above on the rationale of the Color-Word Test, the constricted-flexible control principle seems to involve attributes of ego organization different from those involved in the field-articulation principle.

Before considering results pertinent to Hypotheses 2 and 3, which concern the relevance of the field-articulation principle to performances in tests of the flexibility of closure and spatial relations and orientation abilities, it may be well to examine relationships between the scores of the four tests used to represent these two abilities. This is particularly important since examination of these tests suggested that those representing the flexibility of closure

Table 1

PEARSON CORRELATIONS BETWEEN FIELD-ARTICULATION SCORES (CC 1, CC 2)

AND SCORES FOR CONSTRICTED-FLEXIBLE CONTROL (CC 3, CC 4)

	CC 2. Rod and Frame: Average Error, Total Test	CC 3: Color-Word: Interference	CC 4. Size Estimation: Constant Error, Figured Disk[1]
CC 1. Embedded Figures: Mean Log Time (N = 46)	.44**	-.13	.11
CC 2. Rod and Frame: Average Error, Total Test (N = 63)		.01	-.20
CC 3. Color-Word: Interference (N = 63)			.08

**$p < .01$, one-tailed test.

[1]Probably an inadequate measure of constricted-flexible control, as discussed earlier.

ability may have more in common with the Spatial Orientation Test than with the Cards Test. It was suggested above, for example, that the Cards Test introduces aspects of response that are not produced in either the Spatial Orientation Test or in the flexibility of closure or field-articulation tests.

The results presented in Table 2 bear out these assumptions. The Concealed Figures Test score seems more highly correlated with both scores presumed to represent the spatial relations and orientation ability than these scores (derived from the Spatial Orientation and Cards Tests) are correlated with each other. As expected, Concealed Figures and Designs Test scores tend to be more highly correlated with Spatial Orientation Test scores than with Cards Test performances. It seems apparent—even without considering relations to the basic measures of field-articulation used in the present study—that these ability-test performances cluster in a way that represents the operation of a field-articulation principle and that is not explainable on the basis of earlier definitions of either of the abilities. Performances in the Spatial Orientation Test seem to have more in common with Embedded Figures Test performances than with responses to the Cards Test, which introduces other response processes. As suggested in the discussion of its rationale, the Spatial Orientation Test may actually be an unusually difficult embedded figures test that provides one of the best current measures of field-articulation, as this cognitive variable has been conceived of in the present study.[3] Differences between these tests have also been recognized in the ability literature, in which the Cards Test has been said to sample spatial visualization, the Spatial Orientation Test to sample the ability to localize one's position in space.

Now let us turn to relationships between field-articulation scores and scores for the abilities of flexibility of closure and spatial relations and orientation. The correlations in Tables 3 and 4 add further support to the interpretation offered above. In Table 3, all the correlations between field-articulation and flexibility of closure scores are significant. The relationships between field-articulation scores and scores for the spatial relations and orientation ability

---

[3] For further evidence supporting this point, see the factor-analytic results described in Chapter 7.

Table 2

PEARSON CORRELATIONS BETWEEN FLEXIBILITY OF CLOSURE SCORES (A 1, A 2)
AND SCORES FOR SPATIAL RELATIONS AND ORIENTATION (A 3, A 4)

	A 2. Designs: Number Correct ($N = 63$)	A 3. Spatial Orientation: Number Correct ($N = 63$)	A 4. Cards: Number Correc ($N = 63$)
A 1. Concealed Figures: Number Correct	.43***	.50***	.41***
A 2. Designs: Number Correct		.22*	.16
A 3. Spatial Orientation: Number Correct			.29*

*$p < .05$, one-tailed test.

***$p < .001$, one-tailed test.

(Table 4) are even more striking. In the case of the Spatial Orientation Test, which appears (see rationale above) to be a particularly difficult test of the embedded figures type, the correlation with the Embedded Figures Test score ($-.53$) seems higher ($p. < .10$) than the r ($.29$) *between* the two scores presumed to represent the ability. It is also notable that the Cards Test, which has the most obviously unique features of any of the ability tests considered here, is the only one which does not show significant correlations with both field-articulation scores.

The results shown in Tables 2, 3, and 4 provide clear evidence that (a) the field-articulation control principle is relevant to both flexibility of closure and spatial relations and orientation abilities; (b) when considered from the vantage point of the field-articulation principle, distinctions between these supposedly different abilities are not apparent in the present sample; and (c) the response processes elicited by the *pairs* of abilities tests are obviously less homogeneous than has often been assumed.

DISCUSSION OF RESULTS

These results suggest that not only the Concealed Figures Test, but also the Spatial Orientation Test, call into play—first and foremost—the cognitive control of attention subsumed under the field-articulation principle. In the case of the Spatial Orientation Test, only a radical, if rather obvious, reinterpretation of the response processes it elicits makes these results intelligible. The results point up the need for more careful consideration of the response processes involved in ability tests. Finally, they suggest that these abilities are not as distinct in the present study as in many earlier studies. The possibility that this is due to the fact that all our subjects are women, whose cognitive differentiation in this area of functioning is generally less than that of men,[4] is discussed in Chapter 8, which deals with all the findings of the present study in relation to earlier ability studies.

[4] It was possible to compare field-articulation scores for the present sample of women with those of earlier samples of men. As anticipated, their means indicated field-articulation controls less differentiated than those of comparable samples of men.

Table 3

PEARSON CORRELATIONS BETWEEN FIELD-ARTICULATION SCORES (CC 1, CC 2)

AND SCORES FOR FLEXIBILITY OF CLOSURE (A 1, A 2)

	A 1. Concealed Figures: Number Correct	A 2. Designs: Number Correct
CC 1. Embedded Figures: Mean Log Time ($N = 46$)	-.60***	-.29*
CC 2. Rod and Frame: Average Error, Total Test ($N = 63$)	-.39**	-.25*

*$p < .05$, one-tailed test.
**$p < .01$, one-tailed test.
***$p < .001$, one-tailed test.

Table 4

PEARSON CORRELATIONS BETWEEN FIELD-ARTICULATION SCORES (CC 1, CC 2) AND SCORES FOR SPATIAL RELATIONS AND ORIENTATION (A 3, A 4)

	A 3. Spatial Orientation: Number Correct	A 4. Cards: Number Correct
CC 1. Embedded Figures: Mean Log Time ($N = 46$)	-.53***	-.33*
CC 2. Rod and Frame: Average Error, Total Test ($N = 63$)	-.35**	-.04

*$p < .05$, one-tailed test.
**$p < .01$, one-tailed test.
***$p < .001$, one-tailed test.

Our results also link Witkin's findings concerning interpersonal dependence-independence, and other correlates of the field-articulation control, to the notably similar temperamental correlates of flexibility of closure and spatial ability reported by Pemberton (1952a, 1952b) and Barratt (1955).

4

FIELD-ARTICULATION AND THE
ABILITIES OF VERBAL
KNOWLEDGE,
GENERAL REASONING, AND
IDEATIONAL FLUENCY

The hypotheses discussed in the preceding chapter were closely tied to the definition of field-articulation. Although they could be made only after the abilities tests representing flexibility of closure and spatial relations and orientation had been considered from new vantage points which led to reinterpretation of the tests, the confirmatory results are in accord with previous findings concerning the field-articulation principle. In contrast, the hypotheses considered in the present chapter are based upon tentative or not clearly understood findings in previous studies of field-articulation by Witkin et al. (1954), Gardner et al. (1959), Jackson (1957), Crutchfield et al. (1958), and others.

In reporting that subjects who identify embedded figures rapidly obtain relatively high scores on the American Council on Education Psychological Examination, Jackson (1957) stated that "Clearly, there is a need for systematic study of the various intellectual abilities in relation to mode of perception." Gardner et al. (1959) pointed out that a major degree of field-articulation is involved only in certain *subtests* of intelligence scales (e.g., the Block Design, Object Assembly, and Picture Completion subtests of Wechsler's [1958] scales). Witkin (1959) recently reported results for children that support this assumption. He reports that field-independent children (i.e., those adept at field-articulation) achieve significantly higher scores on only some subtests of intelligence scales, not including information, vocabulary, and comprehension subtests. The fact that intellectual abilities of *verbal knowledge* and *general reasoning* have been defined (see French, 1954) allowed further exploration of the hypothesis that field-articulation in adults is differentially involved in the various behaviors often lumped together under the general heading "intelligence."

In the study by Gardner et al. (1959), relationships between performances in the Embedded Figures and Rod and Frame Tests and performances in a free association test suggested that extreme field-articulators may be relatively adept at selecting associations from their internal complexes of possible associations (articulation of an internal field of ideas), as indicated by the relatively great number of responses they produced in the three-minute period following the stimulus words "House" and "Dry." Although other control principles were also associated with productivity in this free association test, these results suggested that field-articulation may be associated with *ideational fluency* in certain situations. For this reason, a test of the ideational fluency ability was included in the present study.

THE VERBAL KNOWLEDGE ABILITY

French (1954, p. 27 f.) has identified this ability as pertinent to "Knowledge and understanding of the English language." He suggests that previous studies of this factor show it to be a "general language knowledge and comprehension factor which will be found in studies involving speakers of any given language, provided the tests are in that language." Vocabulary tests of various kinds have been used to measure this ability, so that it seems to refer quite specifically to the number of words individuals can define, rather than skills in grammar, sentence construction, composition, etc.

Although the subject's responses to the other tests in the present study are presumed to be governed in part by the operation of enduring characteristics of ego organization, the responses themselves are *current* phenomena presumably representing the momentary state of the organism. In contrast, the responses the subject gives to a vocabulary test were acquired and organized prior to the time of testing and are merely "reproduced" at the time of testing. Even when such findings as those of Yacorzynski (1941) are considered, vocabulary is generally refractory to deterioration and to factors such as anxiety, which may be of considerable importance in some of the timed performance tests used in the present study to represent other abilities.

In view of these characteristics of vocabulary, a link to field-articulation could be envisioned only if one presumed (a) that consistent individual differences in the capacity to attend selectively in certain situations begins to emerge rather early in development, and (b) that the aspects of ego organization subsumed under field-articulation somehow determine the intake and organization of information, including knowledge of the meanings of words.

Closer examination of the phenomena generally subsumed under the concept of "memory" may provide a framework for a tentative hypothesis concerning field-articulation and vocabulary. If individuals are characterized by differences in the selectiveness of attention that arise rather early in the course of development, this aspect of their behavior could have implications for the differentiation with which the external world is experienced under certain stimulus conditions and hence could have implications for memory organization. If this were true, one might expect the extreme adult field-articulator to have acquired a relatively large vocabulary in which clear distinctions are maintained between the meanings of related words. It would seem obvious, however, that field-articulation could, at most, be a minor determinant of the acquisition of vocabulary.

The General Reasoning Ability

According to French, this factor represents "The ability to carry out the kind of reasoning required in the solution of mathematics problem tests" (1954, p. 21). He noted that "This definition does not describe the reasoning process involved. The process, however, appears to be separate from mathematics achievement. The name General Reasoning is used because of the tendency for a variety of reasoning tests, including non-mathematical ones, to load this factor" (p. 22).

Bieri, Bradburn, and Galinsky (1958) have reported significant correlations between performances on Witkin's Embedded Figures Test and a measure of mathematical aptitude.

The test selected to represent this factor in the present study (see description below) was the Mathematics Aptitude Test, which requires solution of mathematical problems. An attempt at a detailed rationale of the response processes involved in this test is made following description of the test below. Suffice it to say here that the relevance of field-articulation to "general reasoning" of the kind involved in this test is questionable and that the prediction concerning a relationship between field-articulation measures and a measure of the general reasoning ability was quite tentative.

THE IDEATIONAL FLUENCY ABILITY

This ability factor has been described by French as "The facility to call up ideas wherein quantity and not quality of ideas is emphasized" (1954, p. 13). According to French, "The crucial element in this factor is the ability to produce ideas, while the expression of those ideas in words is not the major element measured" (p. 14). In the construction of tests for this factor—which require the subject to write down "ideas about a given topic as fast as possible" (p. 14)—emphasis has been placed upon quantity; subjects are generally encouraged not to screen their productions. (That a kind of spontaneous screening relevant to equivalence-range preferences occurred in the Thing Categories, or Things Round, Test used in the present study is suggested by some of the results described in Chapter 6.)

An additional statement about this factor by French seems more puzzling: "it is assumed that the variance in the score depends upon the number and extent of the ideas rather than on any aspect of the process of expressing them" (p. 14). This seems to suggest that individuals "have" different numbers of ideas, say about "Things Round" in the test used in the present study, and that the two-and-a-half-minute test provides a measure of the size of each individual's storehouse of ideas. This seems an untenable assumption. It seems likely that various aspects of cognitive organization govern "the process of expressing" ideas and thus help to determine productivity in this test (see, for example, Rapaport, 1958; Piaget, 1936, and Bartlett, 1932).

In respect to the tentative hypothesis offered below, it must be said that the field-articulation principle—if it is relevant to ease of selecting ideas latently present in internal schemata—may find more ready expression in free association tests of the kind used by Gardner et al. (1959) than in tests of ideational fluency. Because the latter tests demand response within a single category defined by the "topic" (although this criterion is actually not used in scoring), they appear much more "structured." Because of the nature of this structuring, individual differences in willingness to depart from strict adherence to the "topic," as well as individual differences in structures that govern the availability of ideas generally, may obscure the effects of field-articulation upon productivity.

In reference to French's assumption concerning the irrelevance of "the process of expressing" ideas to performances in this test, results of the study by Gardner et al. (1959) indicated that at least two cognitive control principles may be associated with productiveness in free association tests. Included among the determinants apparent within the limited scope of that study were fluency in selecting ideas from internal schemata of ideas (field-articulation) and willingness to produce unconventional responses (tolerance for unrealistic experiences).

HYPOTHESES

With the reservations discussed above and in the sections on rationales below, it was tentatively predicted that field-articulation measures would be significantly correlated (negatively, because they are error scores) with single measures of verbal knowledge, general reasoning, and ideational fluency.

TESTS AND MEASURES OF THE THREE ABILITIES

WIDE RANGE VOCABULARY TEST (Verbal Knowledge)

Materials and Procedure

The test consists of fifty items. In each, the subject is required to select from five possibilities the word that *"most nearly* corresponds in meaning to the word at the head of that group" and to circle the number in front of it. This test was designed to sample a wide span of difficulty levels. The easier items appear early in the test, the more difficult items later. A ten-minute time limit was used.

Rationale

This test of verbal knowledge was adapted from the Cooperative Vocabulary Test. This test was used, rather than one of the more difficult vocabulary tests sometimes used to represent this ability, because of the moderate language proficiency assumed to characterize the present sample of subjects.

This test samples the nature of language schemata formed in the course of the individual's development. It seems likely that the number of words an individual can define is the product of a variety of determinants. In presenting a rationale for the comparable Vocabulary subtest of the Wechsler-Bellevue scale, Rapaport et al. (1945, p. 88) offered the following discussion of relationships between three major determinants of vocabulary.

> To state it in an exaggerated form, *vocabulary is primarily de-pendent upon the wealth of early educational environment, and is refractory to improvement by later schooling and life experience.* The evidence for this contention is much more the clinical experience of the authors than statistical. Clinical experience appears to show that the wealth of stimulation and width of horizon open in the childhood home and environment, rather than the extent of schooling and variety of life experience, influence basically the scope of vocabulary. These relationships are in many cases clouded, because schooling and life experience do enlarge vocabulary to some extent; but the authors have been impressed by how many persons of a culturally poor childhood environment remain limited in their vocabulary despite schooling and life experiences of great variety.

These authors also pointed to a fourth determinant: "the specific character of an individual's intellectual functioning" (pp. 88-89), which they conceive of as "embedded into the personality organization" (p. 89), and hence intimately related to character structure, including defense mechanisms and their dysfunctioning. They point out, for example, the limiting effects of strong repression upon the acquisition of vocabulary, and the tendency of obsessive and compulsive persons to acquire as much information, including vocabulary, as possible in the service of defensive aims.

It is possible that even among persons such as our sample of college students, who have roughly comparable experience with language, those who attend in relatively refined ways in the course of everyday experience form relatively differentiated schemata of words and grammatical constructions. In suggesting the possible role of long-standing patterns of attending in the formation of language schemata, we are again pointing to the possibility that attentional strategies could have important effects upon the intake —and hence the differentiation of registration—of everyday experiences.

It seems obvious that many other determinants play a part in the number of words an adult knows and can clearly define. It would appear to be unknown, for example, to what degree special interest in language, in verbal expression as a means of coming to terms with the world, etc., may influence the development of language schemata. But perhaps these are not separate determinants from those pointed to by Rapaport et al.

Score

A 5. *Number correct.* The score for this test is the number of items in which the subject correctly identifies the word most similar to the stimulus word.

MATHEMATICS APTITUDE TEST (General Reasoning)

Materials and Procedure

The test consists of twenty mathematical problems. In each item, the subject is required to circle the correct answer among the five answers listed. The subject is allowed to use the test pages to perform the computations. The time limit is ten minutes.

Rationale

Rapaport et al. (1945, pp. 195-200) have emphasized the importance of concentration—defined as the "focusing of consciousness upon the current topic, by exclusion of other emotional or thought contents" (p. 168)—in arithmetic tests of this general kind. In discussing the Arithmetic subtest of the Wechsler-Bellevue scale they state:

> Arithmetic is considered here a test of concentration, because to pass the items of this subtest . . . the subject—the average person

of *our* civilization—must utilize *patterns* of arithmetical relations ingrained in him. He must reflect on and deliver the answers from the *patterns* that he possesses. Such focusing upon internally or externally, actually or potentially, existing patterns to discover and amend them, is concentration" [p. 195].

Rapaport et al. state that the patterns necessary to solve relatively easy problems may be assumed to be in the "possession" of "the average American adult" (p. 199), but point out that there are, particularly in the case of difficult problems, individual differences in the patterns themselves. Differences in the acquisition of patterns may be even more important in the present test, which includes many relatively difficult algebraic problems.

Rapaport et al. also pointed out that in the case of such difficult items, "lack of experience with the type of task may make concentration insufficient for coping with the problem, and a complicated process of reasoning and concept formation may become a part of solving the task" (pp. 198-199).

Thus, concentration, although directly involved, may be less important in the present test than in easier arithmetic tests.

Rapaport et al. have distinguished between concentration (active, volitional focusing of consciousness) and attention proper, which is conceived of as "effortless, passive, unhampered contact with outside reality—a free receptivity" (p. 168). Although these two aspects of cathexis shade into each other, the distinction helps to clarify the possible relevance here of the particular aspect of concentration subsumed under the field-articulation control principle. We have emphasized the importance of this principle in problems requiring response to particular parts of complex fields. This selectiveness of attention is a special aspect of concentration and may not be identical to the *amount* of free energy available for the solution of such problems as those presented by the Mathematics Aptitude Test. Field-articulation may be important, however, to the subject's achievement of a field of awareness in which clear distinctions are maintained between the elements of a problem (necessary for dealing with relations between them) and in which attention can be directed to different combinations of the elements. Although the prior ingraining of solution patterns and the capacity to concentrate in the more general sense referred to above would seem to be primary determinants of performance in this test, field-articulation could also have some effect upon performance. This possibility may be enhanced by the fact that a time limit is used. The demand for rapid solutions would seem to increase the otherwise minor importance of this principle for the number of problems correctly solved.

Score

A 6. *Number correct*. The score for this test is the number of correct answers circled within the ten-minute time limit.

THING CATEGORIES TEST (Ideational Fluency)

Materials and Procedure

This test of ideational fluency was developed by Cattell. It is sometimes referred to as the "Things Round" Test.

The instruction page contains an example in which the subject is given two "things that are blue" and asked to add others. The instructions then state that he will be given "another category" and that he is to write in two and a half minutes as many words as possible that fit the new category. The test page states that the new category is "round" and continues: "Go ahead and write all the *things that are round or could be called round.*"

Rationale

The subject is required to search his memory for ideas (often images) representing a particular class of objects. Because of the limitation imposed upon response, this type of test seems to elicit a more focused manifestation of "ideational fluency" than a free association procedure in which the subject is asked to report whatever occurs to him.

In the preceding study of cognitive control principles (Gardner et al., 1959), results for female subjects suggested that field-articulation may determine the fluency with which ideas can be selected from larger schemata of potential responses in a free association test. Whether or not field-articulation is as important a determinant in the present test—in which subjects are asked to produce names of objects within a single conceptual realm—is open to question.

As indicated earlier, in the section on the definition of the ability, various aspects of cognitive organization, including the structures called defenses in psychoanalytic theory, obviously play a part in determining a person's ideational behavior. Those who emphasize the collection of information and the manipulation of ideas (e.g., obsessive-compulsive persons) should be able to produce many responses quickly. Those to whom ideational activity is less important, or those in whom conscious ideation is inhibited, should be relatively unproductive.

Since the description of this test by French (1954) makes no special provision for nonround responses, all object names offered by the subjects were included in computing the "ideational fluency" score. It can be inferred that individual differences in willingness to offer nonround objects may interact with other cognitive variables that determine this productiveness score.

Because of the restriction on the kind of response, subjects may consider and reject a number of objects in the course of scanning their memories for "things round." Most subjects in the present study progressed from writing names of round or nearly round objects to objects in less conformance to the criterion, and there were wide individual differences in adherence to the criterion. An average of only 68 per cent of the objects listed by the sixty-three subjects of the present study could be classified as "Round or Usually Round." In view of this finding, an additional score was developed indicating each subject's "Percentage Round."[1]

Scores

A 7. *Number of words.* This score, used in previous ability studies, is the number of words listed.

A 8. *Percentage round.* This additional score was the percentage of the words listed that are actually round or usually round.

RESULTS

Although five of the six correlations in Table 5 are in the predicted direction, only one (between the Embedded Figures Test score and the Wide Range Vocabulary Test score) is significant. Field-articulation thus seems much less important in the abilities defined as verbal knowledge, general reasoning, and ideational fluency than in the abilities discussed in Chapter 3.

[1] Relationships between this score and a criterion score for the equivalence-range principle are discussed in Chapter 6.

Table 5

PEARSON CORRELATIONS BETWEEN FIELD-ARTICULATION SCORES AND
SCORES FOR VERBAL KNOWLEDGE, GENERAL REASONING, AND IDEATIONAL FLUENCY

	A 5. Wide Range Vocabulary: Number Correct	A 6. Mathematics Aptitude: Number Correct	A 7. Thing Categories Number of Words
CC 1. Embedded Figures: Mean Log Time ($N = 46$)	-.32*	-.20	-.14
CC 2. Rod and Frame: Average Error, Total Test ($N = 63$)	-.11	-.15	.00

*$p < .05$, one-tailed test.

DISCUSSION OF RESULTS

These results help to delimit the major area of relevance of the field-articulation control principle. It seems obvious that it is not a "g" factor relevant to all varieties of cognitive behavior. At least in the present sample, it involves cognitive processes largely different from those represented by the abilities called general reasoning and ideational fluency. It seems likely, too, as discussed earlier in this chapter, that field-articulation in adults is much more relevant to some subtests of frequently used "intelligence" scales than to others.

The results presented here, in conjunction with those discussed in Chapter 3 and those of the studies by Gardner (in press) and Gardner et al. (1959), suggest that individuals are characterized by differences in ego organization that can be conceived of as distributed along a number of distinct dimensions. To be extreme in field-articulation is to respond in a predictable fashion to a certain class of adaptive requirements, but not to other classes. When the adaptive situation demands selective attention, field-articulation may be relevant, whether the problem requires the extraction of embedded figures, response to the *surround* while withholding response to irrelevant embedded figures, focusing upon relevant cues in a "spatial orientation" test, selecting relevant ideas in a free association test, or response to relevant cues in one type of classical illusion (Gardner, in press).

It is important to note here that, although field-articulation is specific to a generic class of adaptive situations, it is related to other aspects of personality organization. Witkin et al. (1954), Witkin (1959), Witkin et al. (1959), Linton (1955), Linton and Graham (1959), Crutchfield et al. (1958), and others have provided evidence, for example, that field-articulation is linked to modes of coping with impulses, conceptions of the self, and the patterning of relationships to other persons.

5

LEVELING-SHARPENING, FIELD-ARTICULATION, AND THE ASSOCIATIVE MEMORY ABILITY

The Leveling-Sharpening Principle

The leveling-sharpening control principle was originally formulated to account for relationships between performances in a schematizing test (used also in the present study to measure this cognitive variable) and time-error assimilation effects in vision, audition, and kinesthesis (Holzman, 1954; Holzman and Klein, 1954). Results of these earlier studies and of the recent study of interrelationships between cognitive control principles by Gardner et al. (1959) suggested that the leveling-sharpening control principle should be defined as a dimension of individual consistencies in the degree to which new stimuli and relevant memory traces assimilate to each other. Correlational and factor-analytic results of that study suggested that subjects at the leveling end of score distributions formed relatively undifferentiated memory schemata in a variety of situations involving temporal sequences of stimuli. Subjects at the sharpening extreme seemed to register discrete memories of successive stimulation. In general, sharpeners' impressions of past experiences were "recoverable" in relatively unaltered form, e.g., for purposes of comparison with new stimulation. Individual variations in the differentiation of memory organization were apparent not only in the Schematizing Test and in a kinesthetic time-error test used in earlier studies of leveling-sharpening, but also in a variety of other tests, including a size estimation procedure testing the preservation of memories of the standard stimuli; an aniseikonic lenses test, in which a new perceptual "process" assimilates, to a greater or lesser degree, to traces of previous experience; a free association test; and the Color-Word Test, in which subjects' reading times for colors alone seemed to represent the differentiation of previously formed semantic schemata. Ancillary findings indicated that sharpeners showed relatively little blocking in the free association test used. These findings also seemed to indicate ready availability of the individual memory elements contained in previously formed schemata of ideas and associations, presumably because sharpeners' original registration of experience involved a minimum of assimilation.

Results of two studies (Gardner et al., 1959; Holzman and Gardner, 1959) suggest that subjects classified as extremely "repressive" (in terms of the original psychoanalytic defense mechanism of "secondary" repression formulated by Freud [1915a]), on the basis of response to the Rorschach Test, are nearly always extreme levelers in the Schematizing Test. Not all levelers are characterized by widespread employment of this defense mechanism, however, and this fact has led Holzman and Gardner (1959) and Holzman (1960) to speculate that extreme leveling tendencies may provide the conditions under which repression can become the major defense mechanism employed by a person.

Mathae (1958) has found that brain-damaged persons show significantly more leveling than sharpening. He also found that levelers and sharpeners do not differ in figural aftereffects.

Recent studies have further extended the generality of this control principle. Gardner and Long (1960c, 1960d) have shown that levelers and sharpeners differ predictably in the number and nature of errors made in a memory-drum learning test, when the similarity of the two lists of words learned is high. Gardner and Lohrenz (1960) have demonstrated differences between levelers and sharpeners in the serial reproduction of a story used earlier by Bartlett (1932). Holzman and Gardner (in press) have shown that sharpeners are superior to levelers in their recall of old memories, as well as of memories created in the laboratory (in their recall of the Pied Piper story, sharpeners retained more elements and preserved the core theme, hence the structure of the story, more frequently than levelers).

Gardner and Lohrenz (in preparation) have confirmed the

speculation of Gardner et al. (1959) that susceptibility to assimilation is in part a function of the intensity with which the person cathects stimuli.

In his review of cognitive control studies carried out at The Menninger Foundation, Gardner (1960) has pointed out several of the major conditions necessary for observation of leveling-sharpening. He has also pointed out that this control may be operative in a wide variety of situations, varying from those in which there is obvious similarity between present and prior stimuli (e.g., as between lifted weights in a time-error experiment), to those in which the person experiences the similarity at an unconscious level (as in the spontaneous importation of old memories into a meaningful story or sequence of themes).

LEVELING-SHARPENING AND FIELD-ARTICULATION AS DETERMINANTS OF LEARNING AND RECALL

Gollin and Baron (1954) have shown that the speed with which persons find the simple figures in an embedded figures test is significantly correlated with the number of nonsense syllables they recall, their savings and relearning scores, in conditions of retroactive inhibition. We would suggest that selective attention is involved in the recall of nonsense syllables under these conditions. In such retroactive inhibition experiments, the subject must hypercathect syllables although they are "embedded" in memory schemata containing irrelevant syllables and although the original list of syllables and the interpolated list tend to "mask" each other. Gollin and Baron's findings are thus similar to the finding by Gardner et al. (1959) that subjects high in field-articulation can attend with fluent selectiveness in a free association test, as well as in response to complex stimulus fields *outside* themselves. It should be noted that the field-articulation factor for women in the latter study was *orthogonal to* (independent of) the leveling-sharpening factor, which seems more directly relevant to the nature of memory formation and, possibly, to the consequent stability of memories.

Gardner and Long (in preparation, a) recently performed an experiment that seems to support the earlier findings of Gollin and Baron. In this experiment, subjects were required to write down two lists of words after hearing both lists read three times. Field-articulation measures obtained for these subjects three years earlier from Witkin's Embedded Figures Test were significantly correlated with the number of words recalled, a result similar to that of Gollin and Baron and indicating once again the enduring nature of cognitive controls.

In a related experiment employing the method of anticipation with two lists of highly similar words, Gardner and Long (1960d) have shown that leveling-sharpening controls another facet of performance—the nature and number of errors in the course of learning. A significantly greater percentage of the levelers' anticipations represented "intrusions" of words removed more than one place from the correct position in the list. Sharpeners showed a significantly greater percentage of one-place intrusions. This finding seems to represent greater assimilative interaction on the part of levelers among the whole constellation of words in the course of registration. Gardner and Long (1960c) have noted, however, the relevance to observation of leveling-sharpening of Bergson's (1911) dictum that such rote-learning tests tend to set up *motor* response patterns, whereas other learning and recall experiences lead to the formation of symbolic and representational memories. It seems likely that leveling-sharpening is even more apparent under the latter conditions.

THE ASSOCIATIVE MEMORY ABILITY

This factor, frequently identified in previous ability studies, was described by French as "The ability to commit pairs of items to memory for short periods of time so that given one member of the pair the other can be recalled or recognized" (1954, p. 15). This definition obviously does not involve detailed consideration of the particular processes sampled by tests for this factor. Since the associative memory tests seem to sample aspects of cognitive functioning different from those governed by the leveling-sharpening principle, tests representing these two variables were included largely for exploratory purposes. Whereas the Schematizing Test used to measure leveling-sharpening seems to allow observation of the *interaction* of new perceptual processes and the trace aggregates of related prior experiences, the associative memory tests seem primarily focused upon the rate at which subjects *learn* new material. Findings from the earlier studies of associative memory tests seemed, on an *a priori* basis, to be more closely related to results of studies dealing with the effects of "perceptual organization" upon learning and recall (e.g., Krech and Calvin, 1953; Köhler, 1958) than to results of studies of assimilative interaction. It seemed possible, also, that field-articulation is important to the rapid acquisition of the pairs of stimuli the subject is required to learn in these tests.

HYPOTHESES

With the reservations noted above, significant correlations were tentatively predicted between both leveling-sharpening and field-articulation scores and scores derived from two associative memory tests.

TESTS AND MEASURES OF LEVELING-SHARPENING

THE SCHEMATIZING TEST

Apparatus and Procedure

This test, based on a procedure developed earlier by Hollingworth (1913), has been used to provide measures of leveling-sharpening. Subjects sit in a dark room in desk chairs mounted with small, shielded lamps. Following dark adaptation, they are required to make 150 judgments of the sizes of squares of light ranging from 1.2 to 13.7 inches on a side. The squares are shown individually on a black screen approximately 15 feet from the subjects by means of an automatic projector. Individual squares are exposed for three seconds, with eight-second intervals between exposures. At the beginning of the test, the five smallest squares are shown in ascending order, then in two random orders (Series 1). Without interruption, the smallest square is then removed and a square larger than any previously seen is added. These five squares are then presented in the same order as in Series 1. The presentation of squares proceeds in this fashion through ten series of 15 judgments. The entire test requires about thirty-five minutes.

Rationale

As the sizes of the squares progressively increase, subjects characteristically tend toward underestimation. In past experimentation, extreme levelers have judged the 13.7-inch square, which appears near the end of the test, as being "5 inches" on a side.

Although initial anticipations concerning the progression of sizes can undoubtedly influence performance on this test (as pointed out by Krathwohl and Cronbach, 1956), the major variable determining underestimation of the sizes of larger squares appears to be assimilation among percepts of new squares and the trace aggregate of smaller squares seen earlier. Both examination of earlier results and factor-analytic results of the study by Gardner et al. suggest that the degree to which the subject keeps pace with the trend of increase in the sizes of squares is an inverse function of his susceptibility to the assimilation effects described in detail by Köhler (1923), Lauenstein (1933), Koffka (1935), and others.

In addition to measuring the degree to which subjects keep pace with the gradually increasing sizes of the squares (represented by the "increment error" measure described below), the Schematizing Test measures individual differences in effectiveness of ranking the stimuli within each of the ten series. The "ranking accuracy" score described below was designed to represent this aspect of performance.

Like the degree of increment error, inaccuracy in ranking the sizes of the stimuli may be a function of the degree of assimilation. Accurate ranking requires not only a clear image of the immediately preceding stimulus, but also clear and differentiated memories of a number of earlier stimuli.

Scores

CC 5. *Increment error.* The method of computing this score was described in detail by Gardner et al. (1959). The score consists of the average of the subject's increment errors in each of the last nine of the ten series. The corrected odd-even reliability coefficient for this score was .98 in the present sample.

CC 6. *Ranking accuracy.* This score was also described in detail in the report by Gardner et al. The number of correct placements within the ten series of 15 judgments is divided by the maximum possible number, 150. The corrected odd-reliability coefficient for this score was .90 in the present study.

TESTS AND MEASURES OF ASSOCIATIVE MEMORY

PICTURE-NUMBER TEST

Materials and Procedure

This test is based upon a procedure originally developed by Anne Anastasi. The subject is required to learn as many of twenty-one pairs of pictures and numbers as possible in three minutes and then immediately to record the proper numbers next to the pictures, which are arranged in a new order on the test page. During the three-minute learning period, the subject is allowed only to examine the pairs; no other form of practice is permitted. Each pair consists of a drawing of a common object, such as a pen, a pail, a dog, a shoe, a boat, which appears in one half of a box. The other half of the box contains a two-digit number. The subject is allowed three minutes in which to reproduce the numbers.

Rationale

This test and the companion Word-Number Test have been included in previous ability studies without detailed consideration of the response processes they involve, and therefore the term "associative memory" seems to be only a descriptive appellation.

Rapaport (1942b) has pointed out that memory includes three major groups of processes: those involved in the registration of new stimulation, the interaction of registrations (including assimilation and related effects), and the reproduction of registrations. Each of these groups of processes obviously requires further exploration. It seems likely that the Picture-Number Test is primarily a "rate-of-learning" test. As such, it may involve articulation of the attentional field in the course of registration of new material. Variations in the efficiency with which attention can be directed to partial aspects of complex fields, discussed in Chapter 3 in respect to the field-articulation principle, could thus influence individual performances. Subjects who can direct undivided attention to individual pairs of pictures and numbers and then move on to other picture-number combinations—in contrast to subjects who are distracted by the multiplicity of picture-number combinations—may have the advantage in this test.

In their discussion of performances in the Digit Span subtest of the Wechsler-Bellevue Intelligence Scale, Rapaport et al. (1945) have pointed to the ways in which anxiety can "ruffle" the surface of consciousness and consequently affect the registration of stimulation. These authors referred to anxiety primarily as a symptom of enduring conflicts integral to the individual's personality organization. Anxiety of a less symptomatic nature can be generated in special experimental conditions, such as a demand for speed in learning. Of two subjects with equal anxiety levels in response to this test, the one who applies a relatively systematic strategy of attending to the complex of stimuli would seem to have a particular advantage over the subject given to less differentiated forms of attending. Anxiety may be reduced by the very fact that previously developed skills in selective attention allow the subject to "do something effective" with the stimuli. In contrast, the subject already at sea when confronted with a number of pairs of stimuli and the requirement to learn them rapidly may become even more anxious as the learning period progresses.

The process of reproduction may also involve selective attention of the kind governed by the field-articulation principle. That is, once the subject has effectively registered a certain number of pairs, selective hypercathexis of the numbers associated with particular pictures may be analogous to isolation of simple figures in embedded-figures tests.

Since the subject learns the pairs in sequence, registration could also be affected by the leveling-sharpening principle. Maximum assimilation among newly examined pairs and preceding pairs in the course of learning could lead directly to an undifferentiated memory organization of the pairs and hence to a low recall score.

An aspect of attention not explored fully in the present study —the sheer intensity with which the subject cathects new stimuli— may have even greater effects upon performance than the field-articulation and leveling-sharpening controls referred to above. As noted in Chapter 3, individuals may have typically greater or lesser *amounts* of neutralized energy available for cathexis of new stimulation. Those with relatively large amounts could experience new stimulation with a degree of vividness that in itself leads to superior learning and recall.

Scores

A 9. *Number correct.* The score for this test is the number of pictures correctly numbered on the test page.

A 10. *Percentage incorrect.* An additional score was developed for this test because of its possible relevance to the equivalence-range principle (see Chapter 6). It consisted of the percentage of incorrect answers, a feature of response not taken into account in the usual score.

WORD-NUMBER TEST

Materials and Procedure

In this test, the subject examines twenty word-number pairs for five minutes, in order to learn as many as possible. Immediately following this, he is required to write the appropriate two-digit numbers beside the words, which are arranged in a new order on the test page. Subjects are allowed three minutes for reproduction of the numbers. This test differs from the Picture-Number Test both in the time the subject is allowed for learning and in that the subject is allowed to practice writing the pairs on the page provided for learning.

Rationale

The response processes involved in this test seem similar to those involved in the Picture-Number Test. Here again, it seems possible that attentional variables, including articulation of the attentional field during registration and/or recall of the paired stimuli, may be major determinants of individual differences in the number of correct responses.

Scores

A 11. *Number correct.* The score for this test is the number of words correctly numbered on the test page.

A 12. *Percentage incorrect.* This score was computed in the same way as the additional score for the Picture-Number Test.

RESULTS

It is evident from Table 6 that no significant correlations link leveling-sharpening and associative memory scores.

Table 6

PEARSON CORRELATIONS BETWEEN LEVELING-SHARPENING SCORES

AND SCORES FOR ASSOCIATIVE MEMORY

	CC 6. Schematizing: Ranking Accuracy (N = 63)	A 9. Picture-Number: Number Correct (N = 63)	A 11. Word-Number: Number Correct (N = 63)
CC 5. Schematizing: Increment Error	-.26*		.10
CC 6. Schematizing: Ranking Accuracy		-.18	-.02
A 9. Picture-Number: Number Correct			.55***

*$p < .05$, one tailed test.
***$p < .001$, one-tailed test.

As expected, somewhat stronger relationships obtain (Table 7) between field-articulation and the associative memory scores. Both these results and some of the factor-analytic results (see Chapter 7) can be interpreted as indicating that cognitive structures relevant to attentional selectiveness in certain types of situations are relevant to performance in these associative memory tests.

DISCUSSION OF RESULTS

The relevance of field-articulation to performances in the associative-memory tests indicates that subjects' responses to the Picture-Number and Word-Number Tests are to some degree determined by cognitive structures that influence performances in tests of flexibility of closure and spatial relations and orientation (see Chapters 3 and 7). These findings may serve as a case in point concerning the interpretive advantages of studying abilities in relation to other cognitive variables. The present results suggest that the behaviors sampled in associative-memory tests are in part determined by more general aspects of personality organization than was previously suspected.

Table 7

PEARSON CORRELATIONS BETWEEN FIELD-ARTICULATION SCORES
AND SCORES FOR ASSOCIATIVE MEMORY

	A 9. Picture-Number: Number Correct	A 11. Word-Number: Number Correct
CC 1. Embedded Figures: Mean Log Time ($N = 46$)	-.14	-.38**
CC 2. Rod and Frame: Average Error, Total Test ($N = 63$)	-.21*	-.36**

*$p < .05$, one-tailed test.
**$p < .01$, one-tailed test.

6

EQUIVALENCE RANGE, FIELD-ARTICULATION, AND THE INDUCTION AND DEDUCTION ABILITIES

Examination of relationships between the equivalence-range control principle and the intellectual abilities of *induction* and *deduction* was the most strictly exploratory segment of the present study. Comparison of these three variables was included primarily because all seem to reflect important attributes of concept formation and because they seem, to a limited degree, to involve related response processes. In view of the possible relevance of the field-articulation principle to performances on tests of induction and deduction, relationships concerning this control principle are also considered in this chapter.

CONCEPT FORMATION AND THE EQUIVALENCE-RANGE PRINCIPLE

As Rapaport, Gill, and Schafer (1945, p. 387ff.) have pointed out, concept formation—the aspect of thought functioning representing the belonging-together of ideas—is evident in a wide variety of behavioral phenomena, including naming, dreams, somatic symptoms, and beliefs. It is apparent in both unconscious and conscious thinking (see Freud, 1900, 1911). From the point of view of logic, each concept has a content (the object characteristics determining belongingness) and a realm (all the objects to which the content refers). It is a clinical commonplace that adults vary widely in dif-

79

ferent aspects of concept formation, for example, the level of abstraction they achieve when required to identify the content of a given realm, the flexibility with which they assign different contents to a given realm, and the inclusiveness of the realms they identify as referable to a single content.

Stimulated by such clinical observations and by Klüver's (1936) suggestion that judgments of equivalence may reflect important aspects of personality organization, Gardner (1953) attempted to define a cognitive control principle relevant to individual differences in equivalence ranges (the inclusiveness of conceptual realms). He described a study which seemed to indicate that a meaningful dimension of individual differences is evident in the categorization of objects in a relatively "free" sorting test (Object Sorting Test); a size-constancy test exploring the strictness with which subjects interpret the requirement to match the retinal sizes of circles; a size-constancy test exploring the strictness with which subjects interpret the requirement to make object matches; and a brightness-matching test. In contrast to early studies of some of the other cognitive control principles, this first experiment concerning equivalence-range consistencies was designed to show something of the limits of the generality of the postulated cognitive control principle.

. Following the original exploratory study, experiments by Dickman (1954) and Marrs (1955) helped to indicate the particular kinds of situations to which an equivalence-range control principle may be relevant. In his experiment, which included the original Object Sorting Test, Dickman failed to find predicted relationships between sorting-test performances and responses to a test in which subjects were asked to divide a movie into event units. Marrs, who felt that the total structure of the movie used by Dickman might have limited the display of individual differences in equivalence-range preferences, demonstrated rather strong individual consistencies between performances on the original Object Sorting Test, the alternate form developed by Dickman, a "Behavior Grouping Test," and a "Figure Grouping Test." In the "Behavior Grouping Test," the subject was required to categorize sixty-nine statements describing a variety of everyday behaviors in the way that seemed most congenial to him. In the "Figure Grouping Test," the subject was required to categorize Chinese ideographs. In Marrs's experiment, the instructions, which were nearly identical to those employed by Gardner for the original sorting test, helped to insure relative spontaneity of categorizing. These instructions emphasized that no "right" or "wrong" answers were possible and encouraged the subject to sort the objects "in the way that seems most natural, most logical, and most comfortable." Marrs concluded that consistencies in equivalence-range behaviors can be demonstrated if tests are of roughly the same degree of "structuredness." His results also suggested that these consistencies can be most clearly observed in situations emphasizing judgments, rather than perceptions, of similarity and difference.

The relationship originally observed between the number of groups into which subjects sort a large number of objects and the exactness with which they match retinal sizes was apparently confirmed for female subjects in the study concerned with relationships between cognitive control principles (Gardner et al., 1959). It seemed obvious, however, both from *a priori* consideration of the response processes involved in the Size Constancy Test and from the results themselves, that this procedure by no means provided an ideal measure of equivalence-range propensities. Many other factors must play a part in the matching process. It was suggested in that study that the field-articulation control might play an important role in this test, which requires subjects to distinguish between two "competing" aspects of their experience.

Other findings in the study of relationships between cognitive control principles indicated that narrow-equivalence-range subjects "categorized" their responses to two stimulus words in a free association test in a more restricted way than did broad-equivalence-range subjects. That is, their associations were unusually "close" to the central meanings of the stimulus words. Ancillary findings concerned the relative abstractness and impersonality of their groupings of objects in the Object Sorting Test, in contrast to broad-equivalence-range subjects, who frequently formed groups on the basis of the everyday meanings of objects or their personal experiences with certain objects. In the Rorschach Test, broad-range subjects projected more human and humanlike content into the blots, used color, and experienced human movement more freely than narrow-range subjects.

Sloane (1959; Sloane, Gorlow, and Jackson, in preparation) recently performed an experiment relevant to the core aspect of the original definition of the equivalence-range control principle. Sloane's experiment, which was completed after the collection of data for the present study, indicated consistencies of individual performance in a version of the original Object Sorting Test; paper-and-pencil tests in which the subject sorts the names of objects[1] and descriptions of people; a test in which the subject sorts photographs of human faces; and a test in which the subject sorts drawings of objects.

Although his pretest preparation of subjects for constancy tests may have varied from that in the original study, Sloane's results probably corroborate other findings which suggest that size-constancy tests do not provide adequate equivalence-range measures. Like the studies referred to above, his results indicate that the principle may be most evident in *judgmental* responses to questions of similarity and difference.

A study of individual consistencies in category width by Bruner and Rodriques (described by Bruner, Goodnow, and Austin, 1956) and a subsequent study by Pettigrew (1958) may be relevant to previous work on the equivalence-range principle.

To summarize, previous studies have shown considerable individual consistency in the categorization of various types of stimuli. Some subjects seem content only when very few objects and object properties are included in one category. Others include a wide variety of objects or object properties in groups classified according to single attributes.

THE INDUCTION AND DEDUCTION ABILITIES

According to French (1954, p. 12), the induction ability was originally identified as a single factor in six early studies, including one by Thurstone (see French, 1951). Following this, however, Adkins and Lyerly (1952) and Guilford et al. (1951, 1954, 1955) separated this ability factor into several subfactors. Thus, induction is referred to in the *Manual* (French, 1954) as "Associated abilities involved in the finding of general concepts that will fit sets of data, the forming and trying out of hypotheses" (p. 12). French suggests that the three tests of induction described in the *Manual*

---

[1] In Sloane's study, scores for these paper-and-pencil tests, developed by Clayton and Jackson (in press), showed loadings on an "equivalence range" factor as high as that for a score derived from the sorting of actual objects.

"do not define any single factor, but will tend to cluster in a battery of heterogeneous tests" (p. 12).

The deduction ability appeared as a factor in several of Thurstone's early studies and in studies by Adkins and Lyerly (1952) and Guilford et al. (1951, 1954, 1955). The factor was described by French as representing "The ability to reason from given premises to their necessary conclusion" (1954, p. 10). Syllogistic tests are thought to provide the ideal measures of this factor.

In view of the likelihood that neither induction nor deduction is ever observed independently of the other, these names as applied to these abilities do not seem adequate to designate the response processes that are involved in the two sets of tests. Rapaport, Gill, and Schafer have suggested that concept formation, rather than induction and deduction, is "the basic unit of thought processes, in which induction and deduction occur indivisibly integrated with each other" (1945, p. 391). An attempt will be made below to outline more detailed rationales for these tests than have been offered previously. In the course of these discussions, the interaction of induction and deduction, particularly in the induction tests, will receive further consideration.

HYPOTHESES

Consideration of the response processes elicited by the induction and deduction ability tests (see the rationale sections below) led to the prediction that:

1. Induction-test scores (Letter Grouping and Marks) would be significantly correlated with one of the deduction scores (Reasoning).

2. Induction-test scores would not be significantly correlated with the other deduction score (False Premises).

3. Field-articulation scores would be significantly correlated (negatively because they are "error scores") with the Letter Grouping Test score of induction.

4. Field-articulation test scores would not be significantly correlated with the Marks Test score of induction.

5. Field-articulation test scores would not be significantly correlated with deduction-test scores.

Although no clear-cut prediction about the induction and deduction scores could be made on the basis of previous equivalence-range studies, it was tentatively predicted that:

6. Equivalence-range scores (primarily that derived from the Object Sorting Test) would be significantly correlated with induction and deduction scores (i.e., that narrow-equivalence-range subjects, by virtue of self-imposed limitations upon the heterogeneity of conceptual categories, might entertain fewer "wrong" inductive and deductive hypotheses, and hence achieve successful solutions more rapidly in the timed tests representing the two abilities).

It was also predicted that:

7. Equivalence-range scores would be significantly correlated (negatively in the case of the criterion Object Sorting Test score) with the percentages of incorrect responses given by subjects in the Picture-Number and Word-Number Tests (see Chapter 5).

8. Equivalence-range scores would be significantly correlated (positively in the case of the criterion Object Sorting Test score) with the percentage round score for the Thing Categories Test (see Chapter 4).

TESTS AND MEASURES OF EQUIVALENCE RANGE

OBJECT SORTING TEST

Apparatus and Procedure

Details of the procedure were presented both in the description of the original study (Gardner, 1953) and in the monograph describing the study of relationships between cognitive control principles (Gardner et al., 1959). The subject is required to sort seventy-three common objects "in the way that seems most natural, most logical, and most comfortable" (Gardner, 1953, p. 219). The objects are presented in a random arrangement. There is no time limit. The only restriction on grouping is that all the objects in any group must belong together "for a particular reason," which the subject is required to state after grouping all the objects.

Rationale

As discussed in the study by Gardner et al. (1959), this test seems to involve individual preferences in respect to breadth of categorizing more directly than do concept-formation tests aimed specifically at determining the level of abstraction at which a person characteristically functions. It is an unusually "free" test; the instructions are overtly permissive. The impossibility of achieving correct or incorrect answers is stressed. The subject is strongly encouraged to form the kinds of groups which he "prefers." In earlier studies, the number of groups into which individual subjects sorted the objects, while complying with the demand that each group be accounted for by a single principle, has ranged from three to thirty-three.

Qualitative observations made in previous studies have suggested that subjects who form few groups, as well as subjects who form many groups, may be aware of slight differences in the properties of the objects. The number of groups into which the objects are sorted seems determined not by sensitivity to differences, but by the degree to which the individual is impelled to act upon the differences he observes.

Score

CC 7. *Number of groups.* The score for this test is the number of groups into which the subject categorizes the seventy-three objects. When the subject forms a large group containing distinct subgroups (as indicated in his stated reason for grouping), each identifiable subgroup is counted a separate group. Objects placed by themselves in "groups of one" are also scored as separate groups.

SIZE CONSTANCY TEST

Apparatus and Procedure

This size-constancy procedure was based upon a test used by Thouless (1932a, 1932b). The present test was described in detail by Gardner (1953) and Gardner et al. (1959). The subject is asked to make a retinal match of circles viewed monocularly through a reduction screen. The standard is a circle of white cardboard 39.7 cm. in diameter, at right angles to the subject's line of vision at a distance of 230 cm. Twenty-three circles varying in diameter from 28.8 to 39.7 cm. are presented to the left of the standard at a distance of 172 cm. In the earlier studies, one ascending and one descending series were employed. In the present study, an ADDA order was used.

In contrast to many size-constancy tests used in previous studies, the present test is preceded by a demonstration period in which the experimenter makes sure that the subject has experienced, in an exaggerated instance, the difference between real and apparent size. Thus, preliminary preparation of varying lengths is carried out with different subjects. This preparation period has the effect of producing more accurate retinal matching.

Rationale

The demand to make a retinal match makes it necessary for the subject to distinguish carefully between two aspects of his experience while viewing the standard and comparison circles: (a) their objective sizes; (b) their retinal sizes. The subject's attempt to make a retinal match usually represents a "compromise" between these two aspects. This compromise has been referred to by Thouless (1931, 1932a) as a "phenomenal regression to the 'real' object." To some extent, the degree to which the subject adheres to the criterion of retinal size may represent his equivalence-range preferences. That is, a subject characterized by narrow equivalence range may impose rigid restrictions upon the comparison stimuli he will accept as providing a retinal image "similar or identical" to that of the standard. It seems obvious, however, that response to this test involves a number of other determinants, perhaps including the field-articulation principle, since to perform effectively, the subject must direct attention to one of two "conflicting" aspects of his experience.

In Piaget's formulation concerning the "law of relative centrations" as applied to size constancy (see Piaget and Lambercier, 1943a, 1943b, 1951, 1956; Lambercier, 1946a, 1946b), fixation times upon the standard and comparison stimuli in themselves induce variations in their apparent objective size, which might lead to variations in retinal matching.

Effective performance also requires the maintenance of the set induced in the preliminary training, which directs the subject's attention to the "retinal" sizes of the stimuli. Any tendency for this set to fluctuate in the course of the experiment could reduce the effectiveness of retinal matching.

Score

CC 8. *Mean diameter*. The primary score for this test is the mean diameter of the comparison figure judged "the same" in retinal size as the standard. A low score indicates effective retinal matching. When the subject calls several comparison stimuli "the same" as the standard, the largest figure called "the same" in the ascending trials and the smallest figure called "the same" in the descending trials are used in the computation of this score.

Tests and Measures of Induction

LETTER GROUPING TEST

Materials and Procedure

This test was developed by Thurstone. Each of the thirty items consists of four groups of four letters. The subject's task is to find the rule which accounts for three of the groups and to mark the fourth group, which represents the exception to the rule. The rules may concern the letters included in the groups, the order in which letters are arranged, letters omitted from alphabetical sequences, etc. The time limit is three minutes.

Rationale

Effective response to this test requires that the subject identify the essential similarity between three of the four groups of letters. The subject must form hypotheses concerning the correct realm and its content (induction) and then "check" his hypothesis (deduction) by making sure that the content is appropriate to the three-group realm he is tentatively considering and that the content does not also apply to the fourth group of letters. Only then can he mark with confidence the group representing the exception. It seems likely, especially in the case of more difficult items, that several hypotheses concerning the correct realm and its content may be entertained in the subject's progress toward solution.

The Letter Grouping Test has one feature in common with field-articulation tests that it does not have in common with the Marks Test (also used to represent induction) or with the two tests of deduction. That is, the process of "induction" involved in successful

response requires "extraction" of essentials from a confusing complexity of stimuli. In this test alone of the four tests representing
induction and deduction, the correct *conceptual realm* must first be
delineated. In the other tests, the realm includes all the given
elements. The "extraction" of the correct realm seems to occur at
a higher level of conceptual activity than the "extraction" of simple
from complex figures in the Embedded Figures Test. Nevertheless
it is possible that field-articulation is involved in both these tests.

It also seems possible that narrow-equivalence-range subjects
who demand rather strict agreement in stimuli they are willing to
consider under a single conceptual heading, may move rapidly to
correct solutions in this test. Their insistence upon exact similarity
could play a part in avoidance of the distracting irrelevancies intro-
duced by the discrepant "elements" of the test. There is, however
an essential difference between this test and the sorting tests that
have provided the best indices of the equivalence-range principle
In the former, the *one* similarity to be "discovered" is dictated by
the nature of the item. In the latter, the subject is allowed to *choose*
the similarities upon which he will base his conceptual groupings
Since previous results have indicated that the equivalence-range
principle is most relevant (a) when the subject is free to form
categories and (b) when he is specifically required to express his
preference concerning the inclusiveness of categories, the Letter
Grouping Test may not evoke operation of the principle.

In addition to the aspects of response referred to above, the time
pressure imposed in this test is undoubtedly an important factor
Anxiety induced by the time pressure could be expected to cloud
or "ruffle" the attentional field (see the discussion of the Digit Span
subtest of the Wechsler-Bellevue Test by Rapaport et al., 1945)
Any such reaction on the part of the subject could be presumed to
make the "extraction" of potentially relevant groups of letters and
the checking of hypotheses in this test more difficult and time
consuming.

Score

A 13. *Number correct.* The score for this test is the number of
items correctly marked within the three-minute time limit.

MARKS TEST

Materials and Procedure

This test was also developed by Thurstone. Each of the twenty items consists of six rows of marks (pairs of short, horizontal, parallel lines). In each of the first five rows, the space between one pair of lines is marked (blacked in) according to a rule which the subject must discern. After discovering the rule by examining the first five rows, the subject must mark the correct pair of lines in the sixth row. Adding to the difficulty of the test is the fact that the grouping of the pairs of parallel lines in one row may be different from that in other rows. The following are examples of the "rules" governing the placement of marks: the third pair of parallel lines from the right; the last pair before the longest open space; the first pair to the right of the first unusually large space between groups of parallel lines. The time limit for this test is eight minutes.

Rationale

The subject must first infer correctly (probably by trial and error involving both induction and deduction) the rule governing the first five rows of an item. That is, he must identify the *content* of the realm. Following this, he must mark the sixth row so that it, too, can be included in the realm.

Although selection of the correct realm from a larger realm is not required, other features of this test make it more difficult than the Letter Grouping Test. This difference in difficulty is reflected in the fact that eight minutes are allowed for solution of twenty items in the present test, whereas only three minutes are allowed for thirty items in the Letter Grouping Test. Contributing to the greater difficulty of this test are the following facts: (a) Unlike the Letter Grouping Test, in which recognition of the identity of letters included in the groups, alphabetical sequences within the groups, etc., can be based on past experience, the materials provided in the present test are unfamiliar. (b) The elements represented by the first five rows of each item are more complex than those of the Letter Grouping Test. Not only the positions of the marks, but the positions of the spaces (of varied sizes) and the relationship between marks and spaces may be involved in successful identification of the content of the realm. (c) Each of the five lines of marks and spaces from which the content of the realm must be induced con tains more units than the four-letter groups of the Letter Grouping Test. (d) The content must be inferred from five, rather than three elements.

Thus, several attributes of this test combine to make it an unusually difficult procedure in which only *relationships* between the positions of the marks and spaces within each of the first five rows can be used to arrive at correct definition of the content of the realm.

The fact that the subject is not free to establish the breadth of the conceptual realm makes it unlikely that the equivalence-range principle is relevant. Although it is possible that subjects who characteristically form narrow conceptual realms may be more facile in active concept formation, nothing in the previous studies of the equivalence-range principle indicates that this is so.

In connection with field-articulation, however, some of the items are analogous to the easier items in Witkin's Embedded Fig ures Test, in that correct solution can apparently be achieved by process of "perceptual recognition." For example, in the first item of the test, the pair of parallel lines marked in each of the first five lines is the second pair in those groups of lines that include three pairs. Accurate identification of the content of the realm can be accomplished almost immediately if attention is directed rapidly and efficiently to the marked pairs, without undue influence from the potentially distracting irrelevant groups and spaces. In the case of most of the other items, however, more complex operations are necessary for solution, and effective perceptual activity alone can not be expected to be a major determinant of the scored aspect of response.

In view of the greater difficulty of items in this test, anxiety induced by it may have even greater effects than in the Letter Grouping Test.

Score

A 14. *Number correct*. The score for this test is the number of items correctly marked within the eight-minute time limit.

Tests and Measures of Deduction

FALSE PREMISES TEST

Materials and Procedure

This test was developed by Thurstone. In each of twenty-five items, the subject is presented with a formal syllogism. Nonsense words are included, so that the items cannot be solved by reference to past experience. Some of the conclusions are correct, others are not. The subject is required to indicate the correct and incorrect conclusions. The test is preceded by a page of instructions including practice items, in which the subject is encouraged to distinguish between "good" and "bad" reasoning. He is told to mark the former + and the latter —. The first item of the test will serve to exemplify the form of the syllogisms: "All sparrows are field mice, and all field mice live two hundred years; therefore all sparrows live two hundred years." The time limit is eight minutes.

Rationale

The approach to concept formation in this test is different from that of either the Object Sorting Test or the induction tests described above. In most of the items, the contents *and* realms of two or more concepts are defined by the initial statements, on the basis of which the subject must judge the adequacy of the conclusion. Adequate evaluation of the degree to which the given realms overlap is probably more important than facility with fairly complex verbal material as a key to successful performance.

In two items, relationships between *attributes* defined in the initial statements provide the raw materials for correct solution. In Item 12, for example, relative size is the key to successful solution: "New York City has a smaller population than Boston, and Boston has a larger population than Philadelphia; therefore Philadelphia has a larger population than New York." This second type of item emphasizes the ability to hold in mind simultaneously the relational attributes presented in the initial statements and to manipulate these in such a way as to provide the proper conclusion.

This test is different from the tests of induction described earlier in one important way. In the tests of induction, a principle must be arrived at, either by a form of "perceptual recognition" or a more complicated form of reasoning. This test of deduction involves consideration of *relationships* of two or more clearly identified concepts. The present test thus seems to involve more complicated processes of concept comparison than do the tests of induction, but involves less active concept formation.

Although it seems possible that subjects who form narrow conceptual realms may be more facile in maintaining the realm distinctions provided by the initial statements, the lack of freedom to define realms and their contents spontaneously may mean that the equivalence-range principle is not relevant here.

This test does not demand the kinds of effective extraction of "embedded" relevant material that seemed an important feature of one of the "induction" tests. It thus seems unlikely that the field-articulation principle is relevant.

Score

A 15. *Number correct.* The score for this test is the number of correct and incorrect conclusions properly identified.

REASONING TEST

Materials and Procedure

This test was also developed by Thurstone. The subject is presented with formal syllogisms. Instead of identifying the correctness or incorrectness of the conclusion, as in the False Premises Test, the subject is required to provide the conclusion himself.[2] In each of the thirty items, two statements, called "Given Facts," are presented at the left of the page. The word "therefore" appears in the middle of the page. At the right of the page, under the heading "Conclusions," the subject is required to fill a blank to indicate a relationship between two elements of the problem about which key statements were made. Among the adjectives used in the items are the following: "less" and "greater"; "heavier" and "lighter"; "as great as" and "greater." Item 1 exemplifies the form of all the items:

D is less than B
E is greater than B   therefore   D is ——————— than E

---

[2] This fact concerning the test used in the present study is at variance with the description offered by French (1954), in which it is stated that the conclusions are provided and the subject must indicate which represent correct inferences

The test items are preceded by a page of instructions containing an example and five practice items. The time limit is six minutes.

Rationale

In contrast to the False Premises Test, in which solution of most of the items depends upon correct assessment of the relative inclusiveness of the two or more conceptual realms defined, all of the present items require the subject to deal with "equal to," "more than," or "less than" relationships between the three "elements" of the problem. This test focuses more directly than the False Premises Test upon subjects' facility in comparing *quantitative* relationships between the elements of the problems. The fact that the second of the two statements in the various items may involve relationships between different combinations of the elements prevents the subject from adopting a "pattern" of approach that will accelerate his solutions as he progresses through the test.

It is important to note here a similarity shared by this test with the induction tests but not with the False Premises Test. The False Premises Test involves facility in comparing the *relative inclusiveness* of two or more given realms. The other three tests do not involve this kind of comparison. Rather, they involve relational thinking concerning *attributes* of given realms or elements within realms. Recognition of the essential attributes determining the "belongingness" of items leads, in the Letter Grouping Test, to correct identification of the content governing inclusion of three elements in a realm and, in the Marks Test, to correct identification of the content characteristics of the first five rows. In the Reasoning Test, the subject is forced to deal with relationships between quantitative attributes of otherwise undefined concepts, the contents of which are identified only by letters. Although the Reasoning Test places emphasis upon relationships between *attributes* of concepts, whereas the induction tests emphasize relationships between *elements* to be included in the realms of concepts, the thought processes involved in these three tests seem analogous. This consideration of the aspects of conceptual behavior elicited by these induction and deduction tests suggests that the Reasoning Test may have much more in common with the induction tests than does the False Premises Test.

Effective performance seems to require that the subject hold the given relationships in clear and unvarying form in the attentional field and compare them with facility. The test does not sample the characteristic breadth of subjects' equivalence ranges.

Score

A 16. *Number correct.* The score for this test is the number of correct conclusions the subject reaches.

RESULTS

The correlations in Table 8 seem to support the predictions concerning the ability tests said to measure induction and deduction. Significant correlations link the induction tests with one of the deduction tests (the Reasoning Test), but not with the other (the False Premises Test), in accordance with Hypotheses 1 and 2. It would thus appear that the distinction between induction and deduction made in previous ability studies is blurred in the present study along lines suggested by detailed consideration of the aspects of conceptualization involved in these tests.

Although significant, the correlation between the two induction scores and the correlation between the two deduction scores are also somewhat lower than would be expected if but one factor were involved in each pair of measures. French (1954), on the basis of a number of studies of reasoning behaviors, has noted that the induction tests probably do not represent a single factor. The present results support this statement.

Important differences between the Letter Grouping and Marks Tests (induction) are suggested by their correlations with field-articulation scores (Table 9). The correlations of the Letter Grouping score with both the field-articulation scores are in the expected direction and suggest that subjects characterized by a high degree of selectiveness in attention (see Chapter 3) are more effective performers in this ability test, but not in the other test of induction (Hypotheses 3 and 4). The correlation of the Letter Grouping score with the solution time score for the Embedded Figures Test $(-.44)$ is somewhat higher $(p < .30)$ than the r between it and the Marks Test $(.26)$.

As anticipated (Hypothesis 5), field-articulation does not appear to be associated with performance in the deduction tests (Table

Table 8

PEARSON CORRELATIONS BETWEEN INDUCTION (I)

AND DEDUCTION (D) SCORES

	A 14. Marks: Number Correct (I) (N = 63)	A 15. False Premises: Number Correct (D) (N = 63)	A 16. Reasoning: Number Correct (D) (N = 63)
A 13. Letter Grouping: Number Correct (I)	.26*	.19	.30**
A 14. Marks: Number Correct (I)		.18	.39**
A 15. False Premises: Number Correct (D)			.29*

*$p < .05$, one tailed test.
**$p < .01$, one-tailed test.

Table 9

PEARSON CORRELATIONS BETWEEN FIELD-ARTICULATION
AND INDUCTION SCORES

	CC 2. Rod and Frame: Average Error, Total Test	A 13. Letter Grouping: Number Correct	A 14. Marks: Number Correct
CC 1. Embedded Figures: Mean Log Time ($N = 46$)	.44**	-.44**	-.08
CC 2. Rod and Frame: Average Error, Total Test ($N = 63$)		-.17	-.06

**$p < .01$, one-tailed test.

10). It is interesting, however, that one of the correlations with the False Premises Test score approaches significance ($p < .10$, one-tailed test). Perhaps successful performance depends, to a minor degree, upon the subject's holding the given conceptual realms in a clearly articulated attentional field. It could be speculated that if subjects were allowed to look only once at the statements defining the realms, rather than being permitted to replenish lost distinctions between the realms by re-examining the statements, individual differences in field-articulation might have a greater effect upon performance.

The lack of correlation (Table 11) between performances in the Size Constancy Test and the Object Sorting Test (which has demonstrated its value as a criterion measure of equivalence range in several previous experiments) suggests that this constancy test does not effectively sample the equivalence-range control. It seems obvious that other sorting tests should be used in future studies to provide additional criterion measures of the equivalence-range principle.

The other correlations in Tables 11 and 12 indicate that the tentatively predicted relationships between performances on the Object Sorting Test and induction and deduction tests (Hypothesis 6) are not present. The relative structuredness of the ability tests and their focus upon *relationships* between realms and their attributes seem to provide information about aspects of conceptual behavior distinctly different from those involved in sorting tests.

It was tentatively predicted that narrowness of equivalence range (as indicated primarily by the Object Sorting Test score) would limit the production of "incorrect" answers in the two associative memory tests described in Chapter 5 (Hypothesis 7) and lead to production of a high percentage of things actually round in the ideational fluency test described in Chapter 4 (Hypothesis 8). The first of these hypotheses could not be given an adequate test. The "percentage incorrect" scores for the Picture-Number and Word-Number Tests were correlated $- .73$, $p < .001$, and $- .83$, $p < .001$, with the numbers of correct responses to these tests. This suggests that the "percentage incorrect" may have been a function of the primary determinants of effective performance, rather than equivalence-range preferences. The prediction to the homogeneity of spontaneously delimited conceptual realms in the Thing Cate-

Table 10

PEARSON CORRELATIONS BETWEEN
FIELD-ARTICULATION AND DEDUCTION SCORES

	A 15. False Premises: Number Correct	A 16. Reasoning: Number Correct
CC 1. Embedded Figures: Mean Log Time (N = 46)	-.14	-.07
CC 2. Rod and Frame: Average Error, Total Test (N = 63)	-.19	-.06

Table 11

PEARSON CORRELATIONS BETWEEN

EQUIVALENCE-RANGE AND INDUCTION SCORES

	CC 8. Size Constancy: Mean Diameter ($N = 63$)	A 13. Letter Grouping: Number Correct ($N = 63$)	A 14. Marks: Number Correct ($N = 63$)
CC 7. Object Sorting: Number of Groups	-.07	-.18	.11
CC 8. Size Constancy: Mean Diameter		-.13	-.24

Table 12

PEARSON CORRELATIONS BETWEEN

EQUIVALENCE-RANGE AND DEDUCTION SCORES

	A 15. False Premises: Number Correct (N = 63)	A 16. Reasoning: Number Correct (N = 63)
CC 7. Object Sorting: Number of Groups	-.00	-.05
CC 8. Size Constancy: Mean Diameter	.06	-.10

gories Test is confirmed ($r = .25$, $p < .05$, one-tailed test) for the Object Sorting Test score, presumed to be the only adequate equivalence-range score in the present study. (The percentage-round score was correlated only .02 with the number of words produced.)

ANALYSIS OF LEVELS OF ABSTRACTION

The Object Sorting Test can provide not only a measure of equivalence range, but also a measure of the level of abstraction at which the subject responds. In view of the possible relevance of level of abstraction to the induction and deduction scores dealt with in this chapter, and the general reasoning score discussed in Chapter 4, among others, an additional analysis was made of relations between abstraction scores and all the control principle and ability measures included in the study.[3]

The subject's reason for placing each group of items together in the Object Sorting Test was scored as conceptual (CD), functional (FD), or concrete (C), following the method described by Rapaport et al. (1945, Vol. I). Two scores were derived for each subject: Percentage Conceptual: $CD/(CD + FD + C)$; and Percentage Conceptual or Functional: $(CD + FD)/(CD + FD + C)$. Correlations between these two scores and all major scores were then obtained.

In contrast to the expectation that at least the reasoning-ability scores would be related to these abstraction scores, only one of forty-four correlations reached significance, and this was most likely a chance result. Either these abstraction scores are not adequate, or this variable is quite unimportant to performance in all these tests.

DISCUSSION OF RESULTS

The findings described in the present chapter suggest that the equivalence-range principle is relevant to a particular aspect of concept formation—the inclusiveness of conceptual realms de-

[3] This subsequent analysis was done by the first author, assisted by Mr. Robert Schoen.

limited under relatively "free" conditions—whereas the induction and deduction abilities (at least as measured by the tests used) involve several other aspects of conceptual behavior. The results seem to indicate that facility in comparing the relative inclusiveness of given realms, or in comparing attributes of concepts in relation to each other, and facility in "extracting" principles which define realms when only one correct solution is possible cannot be predicted from knowledge of preferential realm size. It would appear, however, that individual consistencies may be discernible in different tests focused upon the same aspect of conceptualization.

In those tests in which articulation of a stimulus field by means of selective attention is necessary for active concept formation, particularly the Letter Grouping Test, operation of the field-articulation control is apparent. It is important to note here the specificity of this finding. That is, in the conceptual behaviors sampled in the present study, field-articulation seems important only when direction of attention to relevant aspects of stimulus fields is a test requirement. The present result, like those described in Chapter 4, thus seems to indicate that field-articulation is relevant to a single, generic adaptive requirement.

The logical analysis of response processes in the induction and deduction tests revealed a complex of relationships that break down the arbitrary distinction implied by these designations. The results seem to confirm some of the major assumptions derived from these rationales. This group of findings, like those discussed in Chapters 3 and 4, seems to point up an inherent inadequacy of overly empirical approaches to the isolation of the structures involved in adaptive behavior. As a rule, this kind of approach is based upon too-ready acceptance of previously devised tests and relations between measures derived from them. Too little emphasis is given to the processes involved in the test behaviors and the hypotheses they lead to. A strictly "empirical" approach could yield adequate evidence of the "mental structures" governing conceptualization only if all possible variations of the psychological processes involved in conceptual behaviors were represented by a battery of tests.

Although of several kinds, the conceptual behaviors observed in the present study by no means adequately represent even the limited segment of conceptualization that can be observed in psychological tests. Obvious omissions include tests in which past experience, particularly in the form of verbal stereotypes, can govern responses to questions of similarity and difference, and tests that focus more directly upon the varied conceptual "levels" at which individuals characteristically function.

7

INDIVIDUAL CONSISTENCIES IN COGNITION

The major hypotheses stated in Chapter 3 implied that if correlations among the cognitive control and ability measures were factor analyzed, a relatively strong factor of field-articulation would emerge which had high loadings for Witkin's procedures and for tests of flexibility of closure and spatial relations and orientation. The expected appearance of high loadings on a single factor for both Witkin's Embedded Figures and Rod and Frame Tests can in itself be construed as further evidence of the operation of such a general principle of cognitive organization. The variance these tests have in common may possibly be accounted for in terms of ego structures governing the selectiveness of attention in a wide variety of situations. The same formulation would seem on even firmer ground if such a field-articulation factor also had the anticipated loadings on tests of the two abilities.

The attempts in Chapters 3 to 6 to develop rationales for other procedures suggested additional tentative predictions concerning the test performances considered in this study. It seemed likely, for example, that tests representing associative memory focus primarily upon "intake" processes, including relevant attentional behaviors, and deal only secondarily with the interaction of present perception and traces of previous experiences in the key learning periods. The limited groups of correlational results discussed in Chapters 3 and 5 seemed to support this general inference, drawn from consideration of the response processes invoked by tests of field-articulation, leveling-sharpening, and associative memory.

In such studies as the present one, factor analysis has the additional virtue of allowing unanticipated clusters of scores to emerge that could provide further evidence of individual consistencies in cognitive behavior. Thus, the two factor analyses described in this chapter can be considered both hypothesis-testing and exploratory approaches to the data of the present study. No attempt was made to rotate any of the factors to conform to hypotheses concerning either the cognitive controls or the ability variables.

A FACTOR ANALYSIS OF CORRELATIONS BETWEEN THE TWO BATTERIES OF TESTS

The first factor analysis employed Tucker's (1958) interbattery method,[1] an adjusted principal axis solution that deals only with correlations *between* the scores of the two batteries of tests. The eight cognitive control scores were grouped together as one battery, and the sixteen scores derived from ability tests (thirteen standard and three additional scores) were grouped as a second battery. Fifteen scores from the Edwards Personal Preference Schedule, designed to represent fifteen needs conceptualized by Murray et al. (1938), were added to this second battery, as was the score for socioeconomic status derived from Gough's (1949) Home Index. The complete matrix of intercorrelations among scores included in the present study is given in Appendix A.

The correlations of scores in the first battery with those in the second were analyzed by the interbattery method. Only those factors that are *common* to the two batteries are extracted by this method; variance specific to each battery is not treated. The mere extraction of any significant factors by this method supports our general hypothesis concerning the existence of variance common to cognitive controls and intellectual abilities. The three factors extracted by the interbattery method were subjected to orthogonal rotation by means of the normal varimax analytical solution developed by Kaiser (1958).[2] Results of this interbattery analysis appear in Appendix B.

---

[1] The authors wish to thank Dr. Ledyard R Tucker for his helpful advice on this stage of the analysis.

[2] The IBM 650 program used for the normal varimax rotational procedure was developed by Mr. Donald Lamphiear and Dr. Steven G. Vandenberg of the University of Michigan. We are indebted to Dr. Vandenberg for apprising us of this program.

Factor I can be interpreted in terms of the operation of field-articulation, with high factor scores indicating low articulation. Factor II seems primarily to reflect the cognitive control of leveling-sharpening, with high factor scores indicating leveling, although the association of maximum assimilation effects with poor perform-ances in the Mathematics Aptitude Test (general reasoning) was unanticipated and remains difficult to understand. Although the sparsity of significant correlations involving the Edwards test scores (see Appendix A) suggests that factor loadings for them should probably be accepted tentatively, the Factor I and II loadings seem to indicate that low field-articulation is associated with low achieve-ment need (see also Wertheim and Mednick, 1958, in this connec-tion) and that the leveling extreme of the leveling-sharpening prin-ciple is associated with low achievement, high abasement, and (somewhat incongruously) high endurance. Examination of corre-lations among scores with loadings above .30 on this factor shows that the two leveling-sharpening scores are related (one correlation plus, one minus in each case) to each of the other scores. The Mathematics Aptitude Test is essentially uncorrelated with the three Edwards test scores. Factor III, which involves many of the measures defining Factor I, appears to be a conglomerate, second-order factor accounting primarily for intercorrelations among the abilities.

In view of the similarity of these results to those of the subsequent principal components analysis, no attempt will be made at detailed interpretation of the interbattery factors. The interested reader can compare results of the two factor analyses by examining the factor loadings in Appendices B and C. A substantial amount of common variance exists between cognitive control principles and intellectual abilities. The largest factor provides evidence of the generality of field-articulation as a determinant of response in a group of tasks that are superficially dissimilar but may be generically similar. For example, an important segment of the response processes determin-ing scores for the intellectual ability of spatial relations and orien-tation may be governed by a cognitive organizing principle that determines the degree of articulation of experience in a much wider variety of situations.

A Factor Analysis of All the Correlations for the Two Batteries of Tests

Following the interbattery analysis, the fifteen scores from the Edwards Personal Preference Schedule, the percentage incorrect scores from the associative memory tests (variables A 10 and A 12), and the Gough Home Index were eliminated from the battery. Intercorrelations among the remaining twenty-two scores were then factor analyzed by the method of principal components (Thurstone, 1947). This second analysis had the following advantages for the purposes of the present study: (a) it allowed each of the cognitive control and ability scores to find its place in the entire matrix of major scores; and (b) it included the possibility that the strength of relations between the extensively studied ability measures would pull apart members of the two pairs of cognitive control measures considered most adequate and representative (those for field-articulation and leveling-sharpening). The present study was designed primarily to ascertain whether common variance existed between cognitive control principles and intellectual abilities and to make it possible to peruse the nature of any common cognitive structures uncovered. The experimental design was adequate for this purpose and for the attendant application of the interbattery method of factor analysis. From the standpoint of traditional factor analysis, representation of the ability factors of verbal knowledge, general reasoning, and ideational fluency by single tests may be considered a deficiency in design. Since ability factors are correlated, we could thus anticipate the emergence of factors generated primarily by variance common to several ability factors in the second analysis. It should be pointed out here, however, that verbal knowledge, general reasoning, and ideational fluency were not the primary focus of our predictions and that the abilities we are primarily concerned with here, like the control principles, could appear in the space as doublets.

In the procedure used, a fairly precise estimation of communalities was obtained; beginning with zero in the diagonal cells, four principal components iterations were performed with successively refined communality estimates before the final unrotated factors were extracted.[3] In this comprehensive analysis of relations among the two groups of measures, Factors I and II, identifiable as field-articulation and leveling-sharpening, emerged even more clearly and in closer conformance to anticipation than in the interbattery analysis. This was true of loadings obtained in both orthogonal and oblique rotations.

Six factors were extracted (Appendix C). These factors were rotated by the normal varimax procedure and by the oblimax procedure developed by Pinzka and Saunders (1954).[4] From the standpoint of interpretation, the normal varimax factors and the oblimax factors are remarkably similar. (Factors I and II in both orthogonal and oblique orientations are also generally similar to those obtained in the interbattery analysis.) The detailed interpretations below are based upon the oblimax rotations. No essential changes in interpretation would have been entailed by use of the varimax loadings.

REFERENCE FACTORS, OBLIMAX ROTATION

FACTOR I
FIELD-ARTICULATION

Score	Loading
CC 1. Embedded Figures: Mean Log Time	−.80
A 1. Concealed Figures: Number Correct	.56
CC 2. Rod and Frame: Average Error, Total Test	−.48
A 2. Designs: Number Correct	.39
A 3. Spatial Orientation: Number Correct	.38
CC 8. Size Constancy: Mean Diameter	−.36
A 13. Letter Grouping: Number Correct	.34

This factor may be interpreted in terms of field-articulation. In accordance with the interpretation of this cognitive control principle offered in Chapter 3, it may represent facility in selective attention in situations that contain compelling relevant and irrele-

---

[3] The authors wish to thank Dr. David R. Saunders for his help and advice at this stage of the analysis.

[4] We are indebted to Dr. Henry F. Kaiser of the University of Illinois for his assistance with oblimax rotations of factors extracted in the present study. Dr. Kaiser also compared the normal varimax loadings obtained with the IBM 650 program to those obtained with the normal varimax program he has developed for the Illiac computer. These programs produced closely similar results when used with the factor loadings in the principal components solution.

vant cues. In the orthogonal varimax rotation, this factor accounts for a greater percentage of the common variance than any of the others[5] and corresponds closely to the hypotheses listed in Chapter 3. It is also directly in line with the *a priori* rationales developed for the abilities of "flexibility of closure," "spatial relations and orientation," and "induction." Although loadings for individual tests vary somewhat, this dimension is comparable to the field-articulation factors evident (as Factor I in each case) in the inter-battery analysis and in the loadings obtained by the normal varimax rotational procedure (see Appendices B and C).

Persons adept at selective attention in the presence of distracting cues quickly find the simple figures in Witkin's Embedded Figures Test (CC 1) and in the Concealed Figures Test (A 1). More important for the generality of this principle, they are also adept in the cross-modality selectiveness of attention required for low-error performances in Witkin's Rod and Frame Test (CC 2). The Designs Test (A 2) is another embedded-figures task which invokes the field-articulation principle.

This factor cannot be interpreted as a "spatial orientation" factor. In fact, the clustering of scores here once again raises the question whether the descriptive labels previously assigned to factors containing such tests as spatial orientation are relevant to the primary response processes involved.

As noted in Chapter 3, the Spatial Orientation Test (A 3) can be considered an unusually difficult embedded-figures test, and persons adept at field-articulation are predictably effective. This test does not have high loadings on any of the other five factors, although it does load $-.31$ on Factor III in the varimax rotation. The loadings on Factor I for the two measures of flexibility of closure (A 1 and A 2) and only one measure of spatial relations and orientation (A 3) follow directly from the nature of the response processes, as discussed in Chapter 3.

The Size Constancy Test score (see Chapter 6) in part represents the subject's facility in directing attention to one of two competing aspects of experience, and its loading here offers further evidence of the generality of field-articulation.

As noted in Chapter 6, the Letter Grouping Test (A 13) alone

---

[5] Of the four factors interpreted, III was the next largest, followed by IV and II.

of the "inductive" and "deductive" reasoning procedures used in the present study requires the "extraction" of essential elements from a confusing complexity of stimuli for successful solution. This aspect of response to the test apparently involves the field-articulation principle.

It is interesting to note that *single* measures of the separate abilities of spatial relations and orientation and induction have high loadings for this factor. It thus seems likely here—as it appeared to be in the discussion of rationales for these procedures—that performances on the pairs of ability tests used in the present study are differentially determined by the field-articulation principle.

It was pointed out in Chapter 5 that tests for associative memory may call the field-articulation control into play. In the present oblique rotation, these scores (A 9, A 11) do not have defining loadings. In view of the susceptibility of oblique solutions to unique features of samples of subjects and samples of tests in particular studies (see Guilford's [1956] comments on this point), it is important to note that both these scores did have defining loadings on the comparable Factor I obtained by the orthogonal normal varimax procedure. In that solution, the loadings were .33 and .48 for the Picture-Number and Word-Number scores, respectively. These scores had even higher loadings (—.46 and —.63) on the field-articulation factor obtained in the normal varimax rotation of interbattery factors.

FACTOR II
LEVELING-SHARPENING

Score	Loading
CC 5. Schematizing: Increment Error	—.69
CC 8. Size Constancy: Mean Diameter	—.43
A 9. Picture-Number: Number Correct	—.38
CC 6. Schematizing: Ranking Accuracy	.35

This factor appears to reflect leveling-sharpening and conforms to anticipations concerning this principle based on previous work (see Chapter 5). It is assumed to reflect the degree of assimilation among processes representing new stimulation and trace aggregates of prior stimulation.

As in earlier experiments, minimal lagging behind the trend of increase in the sizes of squares in the Schematizing Test (CC 5) is associated with high ranking accuracy (CC 6). Since earlier squares are generally smaller, low assimilation leads to little progressive underestimation of the sizes of the larger squares, and hence to small increment errors. High ranking accuracy is also presumed to be in part a function of low assimilation.

The fact that accurate retinal matching in the Size Constancy Test (CC 8) is associated with low assimilation (sharpening) in the Schematizing Test is not easily understood. Perhaps low assimilation of impressions of the generally smaller comparison stimuli and the standard stimulus as the subject looks from one to the other in this test leads sharpeners to relative accuracy of retinal matching.

The association of low assimilation (sharpening) in these tests with low numbers of correct responses in the Picture-Number Test (A 9) is puzzling. As discussed in Chapter 5, sharpening was expected—if anything—to be associated with relatively effective performance on this test. Perhaps this relatively low loading should not be taken too seriously, since the correlations between the Schematizing and Picture-Number scores are essentially of zero order (see Table 6, Chapter 5). The contrast between the loadings for associative memory tests on Factor I as obtained in orthogonal and oblique rotations suggests the need for research to delineate further the response processes involved in associative memory tests.

FACTOR III

Score	Loading
A 16. Reasoning: Number Correct	−.71
A 14. Marks: Number Correct	−.47
A 4. Cards: Number Correct	−.42

FACTOR IV

Score	Loading
A 5. Wide Range Vocabulary: Number Correct	.68
A 6. Mathematics Aptitude: Number Correct	.47
A 11. Word-Number: Number Correct	.46
A 9. Picture-Number: Number Correct	.38

Factors III and IV apparently emerge as second-order factors generated by intercorrelations among abilities. This interpretation of Factor III is embarrassed, however, by the fact that pairs of tests were included for each of the abilities represented here (induction, deduction, and spatial relations and orientation), whereas only a single test of each has a defining loading. Factor III could, however, be a general reasoning factor. The inclusion of the Cards Test highlights the possible reasoning component of this test and is consistent with the rationale presented in Chapter 3, in which it was pointed out that Cards seems to involve response processes different from those of the spatial orientation test. Factor IV appears to be a second-order factor combining verbal skills, general reasoning, and the response processes involved in the associative memory tests. The appearance of this factor may have been determined by the inclusion of single tests of verbal knowledge and general reasoning.

Factors V and VI appear to be quite specific, with the primary loading on the former belonging to Object Sorting: Number of Groups, and on the latter to Thing Categories: Percentage Round.

DISCUSSION OF THE FACTOR-ANALYTIC RESULTS

As anticipated on the basis of the original hypotheses that led to the design and execution of the present study, and on the basis of the rationales developed for the ability tests included here, the field-articulation principle is relevant to performances in tests representing at least four previously defined factorial abilities: flexibility of closure, spatial relations and orientation, associative memory, and inductive reasoning. Although the reasons are less clear, the leveling-sharpening principle may be relevant to performance in tests of associative memory. Thus, important relationships emerge among scores for cognitive control principles and intellectual abilities which, although both are cognitive in nature, have usually been treated separately in research and theory.

Although it can be argued that not enough tests were administered to allow emergence of some of the individual ability factors, it is noteworthy that the members of the *pairs* of ability scores selected from the "Kit" (French, 1954) for the most part produced markedly varying patterns of factor loadings[6] The major exception is the pair of scores presumed to represent associative memory. This finding in itself suggests the necessity, dwelt upon in some detail in Chapters 3 to 6, of reconceptualizing the *response processes*

---

[6] A partial centroid factor analysis of correlations among ability scores alone produced similar results.

previously assumed to be sampled by various ability procedures. And, although the two associative memory tests seem more closely related to each other than members of the other pairs of ability tests, the results also suggest that the term "associative memory" fails to include some of the key response processes.

The factor-analytic results, like the correlational results described in earlier chapters, support the thesis that one cognitive control principle is predictably related to several intellectual abilities. In some cases, e.g., the relation between field-articulation and the flexibility of closure ability, the similarity between the tests is so great as to suggest the value of reconceptualizing the intellectual ability in terms of the broader framework provided by the control principle conception. In other cases, the strikingly different relational patterns of two tests supposedly representing single abilities suggests at least two things: (a) that the "Kit" of ability tests may need revision guided by more careful consideration of the response processes involved in these tests; (b) that the previously defined abilities may arrange themselves differently when included in broader arrays of cognitive behaviors.

The general outcome of the present study suggests that individual procedures previously said to measure particular abilities provide a fertile sample of adaptive behaviors, and that these behaviors involve the differential controlling effects of cognitive structures that guide response in a wider variety of situations. The problem for personality theory, however, is not simply one of exploring relationships between the cognitive consistencies called abilities and other aspects of personality organization. The problem lies, rather, in developing a unified theory of cognitive organization which incorporates the consistencies summarized by the ability conception. Chapter 8 is devoted to a consideration of the implications of our results for the development of such a theory.

8

THEORETICAL IMPLICATIONS
OF THE STUDY

The major finding of the present study is the link between tests of the field-articulation control principle and certain tests of previously defined intellectual abilities. This finding is not an artifact of the factor-analytic methods used. It is apparent in the clustering of related test performances in each of the methods used and in both orthogonal and oblique factor rotations. The puzzling finding is that, in contrast to findings in many earlier studies of abilities, members of the pairs of tests used to sample a particular ability generally do not cluster together in ways that would indicate the presence of the ability presumably being tested in addition to the general field-articulation control. With the exception of the pair of tests selected to represent the ability called associative memory, our subjects' responses to individual members of these pairs of ability tests seem more independent than related. That is, except for their common linkage to the field-articulation principle, responses to these tests seem to represent different aspects of cognitive organization.

The appearance of a general field-articulation factor, and the failure of the specific abilities to appear as discrete entities, raises some important questions concerning the nature of the cognitive structures involved in our subjects' responses. If it were not for the fact that the abilities called flexibility of closure, spatial relations and orientation, etc., have appeared as correlated but distinguishable entities in many previous studies, it might seem that these abilities appear in discrete form only when they are studied within the limited realm of other paper-and-pencil ability tests. In the case of the observed relationship between the field-articulation principle and the flexibility of closure ability, it may be true—as suggested in Chapter 3—that largely identical processes are sampled in the two sets of core tests and that the more broadly conceived control principle is the essential aspect of ego structure determining performance. In view of the fact that embedded figures tests provide core measures of both field-articulation and flexibility of closure, this argument seems quite firmly based. The same thing may or may not be true of the other abilities included in the study, although the rationales developed for the abilities tests suggest that a number of them call into play the structural arrangements of psychological processes subsumed under the field-articulation control.

If the anticipated specific ability factors had appeared in addition to the general field-articulation factor, it could be argued that the response to the relevant ability *tests* is in part governed by the field-articulation principle, but that the ability is still a distinct and independent entity. That this does not appear to be true in the present study may be due to one of the following causes: (a) The relevant ability tests may be primarily field-articulation tests, and the abilities not distinct facets of cognitive organization. (b) The obvious differences between some of the tests previously assumed to represent the same abilities account for their failure to cluster together in factors other than the field-articulation factor; refinement of these tests may yet show that spatial abilities represent additional cognitive structures. (c) Our results may be attributable to the use of only female subjects in the present study. The last of these possibilities seems the most fruitful interpretation of our results and is discussed in greater detail below. The value of this interpretation seems particularly clear in that analysis of correlations between the ability measures alone indicates that separate factors identifiable as flexibility of closure, spatial relations and orientation, etc., do not appear even when these correlations are factor analyzed separately.

As noted earlier, most ability studies have been done with men, who are known to be more adept at field-articulation and to score higher in "spatial" ability tests than women. These earlier findings seem to imply greater structural differentiation in respect to both field-articulation and these specific abilities in the case of male subjects. In the present study, the generality of the field-articulation principle and the absence of these ability factors may result from the fact that our young female subjects are relatively undifferentiated in respect to this cognitive control, and that certain specific abilities are therefore too undifferentiated to be observed as separate entities. Given such a group of women, the control may serve as the major determinant of performances in all these situations. Given a group of men, the field-articulation control may be *linked* to several distinguishable ability factors (perhaps appearing as a second-order factor that in part represents the correlations among these abilities). The conclusion would be obvious: when cognitive organization in this general area is relatively refined, several specific abilities are linked to field-articulation, a general principle of cognitive control relevant to any situation (spatial, verbal, learning, etc.) requiring selective attention in the face of compelling irrelevant cues. This interpretation of the present results gains support from Barratt's (1955) finding that men have several related but distinct "spatial" abilities, whereas women tend to have a *general* and lower-order ability. It can also be considered analogous to the emphasis placed by several students of abilities (e.g., Zimmerman, 1954a, 1954b; Michael, 1954) on the relationship between the levels of difficulty of various ability *tests* (e.g., "spatial" tests) and the ability factors obtained.

Further studies based on the present findings must obviously employ (a) more refined ability tests; (b) larger samples of men, as well as women; (c) larger samples of tests representing the control principles and these abilities.

The rationales developed for ability tests in Chapters 3 to 6 pointed to the fact that tests presumed to represent a single ability frequently include very different response processes. Our results confirm these assumptions. The implication is that the "Kit" of ability tests (French, 1954) must be re-examined, and new tests developed or old tests refined. But how should this be done? On the one hand, it might be argued that tests should be developed— for example, in the area of "spatial" abilities—that provide distinct measures of several such abilities but that are *independent* of field-articulation. This approach would require new process conceptions of these correlated abilities and would involve elimination of some of the major tests used in earlier ability studies, e.g., the Spatial Orientation Test used in the present exploration. We would argue, however, that such an approach overlooks the valuable yield of earlier ability studies and fails to appreciate the likelihood of a hierarchical arrangement of cognitive structures that serve (a) general and (b) relatively specific functions in adaptation.

A more fruitful approach would respect the hierarchical arrangement of cognitive structures by employing the assumption that a general principle of cognitive control, such as field-articulation, may be linked to a *group* of relatively specific abilities. The refinement of reference tests for abilities could then be focused upon the production of clusters of tests that truly sample distinct but *correlated* abilities in this general area of cognitive functioning. We have suggested that the correlations previously observed between several abilities may in part result from their being linked to a general principle of cognitive control, and that the appearance of these abilities as discrete entities is a function of the degree of differentiation of the cognitive structures. We are assuming that when each of these abilities is called into play by the relevant adaptive requirement and stimulus conditions, the control is also called into play. Although this general approach points to the need for some reconceptualization of the "spatial" and other abilities linked to field-articulation, it respects the large body of earlier information concerning these abilities and promises to reveal meaningful links between such abilities and general principles of cognitive organization.

Cattell (e.g., 1945) has postulated that direct and indirect kinds of causative interactions occur between abilities and other aspects of personality organization. It seems possible that such mutual "feedback" also occurs in the developmental emergence of cognitive controls and abilities. For example, generalized facility in selective attention may provide a necessary condition for the differentiation of several linked abilities. Because of their implications for success and gratification in particular classes of situations, specific abilities may contribute to the differentiation of the control principle. Although this formulation rests upon the *assumption* that differentiation in generalized controls and linked abilities go hand in hand, it may be the most appropriate interpretation of our results, particularly when these new findings are viewed in the light of earlier findings in ability studies.

Our interpretation of the present results does not assume that the frequently observed superiority of men over women and boys over girls in field-articulation and several of the linked abilities necessarily represents constitutionally given characteristics of the cognitive apparatus. It seems as likely that these male-female differences are primarily determined by the value our society places upon the development of active, analytical skills on the part of males and the development of relatively passive, nonanalytical orientations on the part of females in response to particular kinds of adaptive requirement which call field-articulation controls into play. At a deeper dynamic level, these differences in test performance may be linked to active, penetrating, "phallic" attitudes of the male and passive, accepting attitudes of the female which have their roots in body images. The developmental emergence of characteristically refined or unrefined selectiveness in attention has other obvious roots in the pattern of identification and/or incorporation characterizing the individual child, including the cognitive behaviors and evaluative attitudes (Witkin, 1959) of the parental figures.

It should be noted here that the process rationale of the field-articulation principle developed by Gardner et al. (1959) and elaborated and applied here can account only for individual variation *common* to tests of field-articulation and the several abilities that may be linked to it. If subsequent studies show that separate abilities linked to field-articulation can be identified in groups of persons whose relevant cognitive structures are highly differentiated, it will still be necessary further to develop *process* rationales for these correlated abilities. In the case of the "spatial" abilities, one of the most obvious ways to approach this problem is through use of Witkin's Rod and Frame Test. The remarkable fact about this test is that it involves the same kind of selective attention and response required in embedded-figures tests, other tests of orientation in space, tests employing certain illusions, particular aspects of learning and recall tests, and response to a wide variety of other superficially different but generically similar situations. The Rod and Frame Test is a much more direct test of spatial orientation under *one* set of conditions than any of the paper-and-pencil ability tests. In fact, further exploration of relations between response to these ability tests and response in situations actually involving spatial orientation is a general requirement, if we are to improve our understanding of these abilities.

As noted in Chapter 1, it may be that not all cognitive controls are related to intellectual abilities. The fact that the field-articulation principle is related to several abilities points, however, to the likelihood that the other abilities, too, will be fully understood only when explored in relation to other aspects of cognitive organization. If such explorations are to lead to effective postulations concerning cognitive structure, they must sample a wide variety of possibly relevant behaviors. These explorations cannot be limited to paper-and-pencil tests, laboratory tests, or even these plus clinical tests. To take an example from studies of leveling-sharpening, which may be linked to the "associative memory" ability, this control has been inferred from responses to a wide variety of situations involving temporal sequences of stimulation and has been shown to be related to the strength and pervasiveness of the defense of repression. It has been explored in The Menninger Foundation Perception Laboratory as a determinant of individual differences in learning and recall; in the formation of memory schemata of the kind given general description by Bartlett (1932); in production of the "importations" described by Paul (1959); and in many other generically similar behaviors. Studies have been made of possible relations between this general principle of cognitive organization and individual differences in the satiation effects described by Köhler and others. The role of this cognitive control, or of cognitive *styles* involving this control, in the experiencing of the self, other persons, and social situations must be further explored. Other important questions concern the effects of leveling-sharpening on the recall of dreams and other drive-close cognitive behaviors, and the importance of attentional variables (e.g., the intensity and clarity of attention, and the centrality or peripherality in the attentional field of new experiences) as determinants of assimilative interaction among new experiences and memories of related earlier experiences. These examples, drawn from a larger body of past and current researches concerning leveling-sharpening, are all necessary for an evaluation of its place in the larger framework of personality organization. In the same way, the more specific ability variables must be examined in the context of extensive and varied samples of behavior before their place in cognitive organization will be adequately understood.

In addition to the need for further studies of relations between field-articulation, leveling-sharpening, and certain abilities, the present study points to the value of studies of cognitive control principles in relation to performances in such intelligence tests as those of Wechsler (1958). Witkin (1959) has shown that, in the case of children, field-articulation measures allow prediction to some of these subtests but not others. These leads are being followed as part of a larger study at The Menninger Foundation that is focused on relations between cognitive controls and performances in a variety of clinical tests; the strength and modes of employment of various defensive structures; and several other aspects of ego organization.

Such programs of exploration of cognitive controls and abilities may be most fruitful if conducted in the context of a general theory that leads one to anticipate the emergence of adaptive structures that are related to other enduring process arrangements, e.g., those controlling the expression of conflicting drives and determining the nature, quality, and modes of expression of affect. There seems little reason to assume that the various cognitive structures emerge from anything but a common matrix of constitutional and experiential determinants. Psychoanalytic theory is fully compatible with this point of view. The ego-psychological assumptions, drawn from psychoanalytic theory, that led to the design and execution of the present study seem to have some distinct advantages for the generation of fruitful hypotheses concerning relationships between consistencies in cognitive behavior and other aspects of personality organization.

9

THE STUDY IN BRIEF

Although a number of earlier studies provided direct or indirect evidence of relationships between intellectual abilities and the general principles of cognitive organization conceptualized as cognitive controls, no full-scale assessment of this hypothesis had been undertaken. The present study was therefore designed to explore relations between four control principles and eight intellectual abilities.

Two laboratory tests developed and used in a number of studies of individual differences by Witkin and his associates provided measures of field-dependence, or as termed here, field-articulation. Results of earlier studies of this aspect of cognition suggest that the *articulation* of experience by means of selective attention to relevant versus compelling irrelevant stimuli may be the key to effective performance in these laboratory procedures. This working hypothesis is based on the assumption that earlier definitions of "field-dependence" as the ability to extract items from *surrounds* is too limited. Persons who can achieve selective attention to stimulus items embedded in conflicting surrounds can also achieve selective attention to the surrounds when required. They can apparently attend selectively in other situations in which such part-whole relationships do not obtain. This selectiveness is, of course, not limited to response to external stimuli; it seems as apparent when the "field" to be attended to consists of memory schemata, some of which are relevant, others compelling but irrelevant, to the task at hand.

This working hypothesis seemed useful in predicting relationship between field-articulation and the ability called "spatial rela- individual variations in several of the intellectual abilities isolated in factor-analytic studies by Thurstone and later students of abilities. This hypothesis allowed prediction, for example, of a relationship between field-articulation and the ability called "spatial relations and orientation." It has been our contention, however, and the results seem to confirm it, that the paper-and-pencil tests commonly used to sample this "spatial" ability are, like Witkin's Rod and Frame Test, not exclusively spatial tests in terms of the total response processes involved but are also heavily saturated with the requirement to attend selectively to relevant versus irrelevant stimuli. "Spatial" and other labels, applied to such tests on the basis of their content, rather than the psychological functions involved, are sometimes incomplete descriptions and may in fact be misleading.

In some instances, the working hypothesis concerning field-articulation allowed prediction to one, but not the other, of two tests supposedly representing the same intellectual ability. These results also point to the need for further studies of the processes sampled by ability tests. Experimental and experimental-correlational studies of this kind that provide more, and more generic, measures of some of the control principles were undertaken following the present study. Current progress in this area has been summarized by Gardner (1960).

In addition to field-articulation, measures of three other dimensions of cognitive control were included for exploratory purposes. These included measures of leveling-sharpening, assumed to represent the characteristic degree to which current percepts and relevant memory traces interact or assimilate in the course of registration of the current percepts and memories; measures of equivalence range, assumed to represent the degree of differentiation in individuals' experiencing of similarity and difference; and measures of constricted-flexible control. In order to assess relationships between the four dimensions of cognitive control and the eight intellectual abilities sampled (flexibility of closure, spatial relations and orientation, verbal knowledge, general reasoning, ideational fluency, associative memory, inductive reasoning, and deductive reasoning), intercorrelations of all the measures were obtained and factor analyzed by two methods. An interbattery factor analysis dealt only with variance common to the two classes of measures—cognitive controls and intellectual abilities. A more comprehensive principal components factor analysis determined the major dimensions of cognitive functioning represented in the correlations within, as well as between, the two classes of measures. In factor-analytic terms, the principal hypothesis was that a field-articulation factor would have loadings both on Witkin's measures and measures representing several intellectual abilities (principally flexibility of closure and spatial relations and orientation) that seem also to involve selective attention. This hypothesis was confirmed. As anticipated, the other three control dimensions seem largely unrelated to intellectual abilities thus far defined.

The present study supports the findings of Gardner et al. (1959) pointing to the *multi*dimensional nature of cognition at the level of organization represented by the control principle constructs. In correlational and factor-analytic terms, the measures used to represent different controls appear remarkably independent of each other: the correlations between controls are low; the factors obtained differ only slightly when rotated by analytical methods that require orthogonality and by a method that allows oblique factor placements.

The major theoretical contribution of the present study derives from the clear evidence that intellectual abilities and cognitive controls are not isolated aspects of cognitive organization but are mutually interrelated. The arbitrary distinction that has sometimes been maintained between intelligence and the broad-scale organization of cognition thus seems inappropriate. A major assumption inherent in the ego-psychological point of view is thus supported by our results. It should be noted here, too, that the selectiveness of attention apparent in response to laboratory tests of field-articulation is in itself but one expression of a more general dimension of individual differences in the articulation of experience that includes, for example, the articulation of conceptions of the self.

Possibly because the present sample was limited to women, some of the intellectual abilities previously identified as separate entities were evident only as representatives of the field-articulation dimension of cognitive organization. Since women in our culture are, on the average, less adept at tasks requiring an analytical, field-articulating approach, the study should be repeated with improved ability and control tests administered to male subjects. In men, some of these abilities may be sufficiently differentiated to appear in a hierarchical relationship to a control principle: that is, linked to the field-articulation principle but evident in their own right as abilities relevant to special classes of adaptive requirements.

Table 13

INTERCORRELATIONS OF FORTY SCORES[a]

	CC 1	CC 2	CC 3
[b]CC 1. Embedded Figures: Mean Log Time			
CC 2. Rod and Frame: Average Error	44		
CC 3. Color-Word: Interference	-13	01	
CC 4. Size Estimation: Constant Error	11	-20	08
CC 5. Schematizing: Increment Error	-03	02	-31
CC 6. Schematizing: Ranking Accuracy	-18	-13	-04
CC 7. Object Sorting: Number of Groups	25	-02	-27
CC 8. Size Constancy: Mean Diameter	36	18	-08
A 1. Concealed Figures: Number Correct	-60	-39	00
A 2. Designs: Number Correct	-29	-25	05
A 3. Spatial Orientation: Number Correct	-53	-35	-08
A 4. Cards: Number Correct	-33	-04	-01
A 5. Wide Range Vocabulary: Number Correct	-32	-11	-02
A 6. Mathematics Aptitude: Number Correct	-20	-15	07
A 7. Thing Categories: Number of Words	-14	00	-01
A 8. Thing Categories: Percentage Round	-22	-06	-20
A 9. Picture-Number: Number Correct	-14	-21	-18
A 10. Picture-Number: Percentage Incorrect	01	00	07
A 11. Word-Number: Number Correct	-38	-36	-09
A 12. Word-Number: Percentage Incorrect	29	30	03
A 13. Letter Grouping: Number Correct	-44	-17	-04
A 14. Marks: Number Correct	-08	-06	-09
A 15. False Premises: Number Correct	-14	-19	-14
A 16. Reasoning: Number Correct	-07	-06	-23
E 1. Achievement	-08	-26	-02
E 2. Deference	18	02	11
E 3. Order	14	-02	-03
E 4. Exhibition	-32	-16	-03
E 5. Autonomy	20	-05	01
E 6. Affiliation	-02	18	-06
E 7. Intraception	-03	11	02
E 8. Succorance	02	03	12
E 9. Dominance	-11	02	02
E 10. Abasement	-06	-07	00
E 11. Nurturance	26	18	08
E 12. Change	01	-02	02
E 13. Endurance	03	-01	00
E 14. Heterosexuality	-17	-02	-05
E 15. Aggression	-04	00	-16
G 1. Home Index	-12	-06	08

[a]Decimal points omitted. $N = 63$ except for CC 1, for which $N = 46$

[b]CC = cognitive control principle measure; A = ability measure; E = Edwards Personal Preference Schedule measure; G = Gough's socioeconomic status measure.

Table 13 (Continued)

	CC 4	CC 5	CC 6	CC 7	CC 8	A 1	A 2	A 3
CC 1.								
CC 2.								
CC 3.								
CC 4.								
CC 5.	04							
CC 6.	02	-26						
CC 7.	-10	02	-08					
CC 8.	01	32	-25	-07				
A 1.	-01	-07	14	-06	-36			
A 2.	09	03	04	-17	-20	43		
A 3.	02	17	-05	-09	-16	50	22	
A 4.	07	-02	-11	-33	-14	41	16	29
A 5.	05	-18	15	-25	-08	16	07	24
A 6.	02	-28	13	04	-15	41	17	30
A 7.	-16	07	-12	-15	-04	04	-03	06
A 8.	-09	13	-15	25	13	-07	-20	12
A 9.	19	11	-18	10	00	19	10	31
A 10.	-08	-02	09	-02	-05	-06	08	-09
A 11.	00	10	-02	05	-10	29	22	21
A 12.	00	-02	00	-02	08	-17	-12	-16
A 13.	05	15	10	-18	-13	42	17	28
A 14.	03	10	06	11	-24	23	05	17
A 15.	03	20	-01	00	06	25	-06	17
A 16.	-04	00	-11	-05	-10	35	10	36
E 1.	00	-17	19	04	-36	17	21	17
E 2.	12	04	-27	13	09	-15	-07	03
E 3.	16	06	-28	14	07	-14	-02	18
E 4.	-03	-07	24	-14	-05	06	05	-09
E 5.	15	-18	00	13	08	05	06	09
E 6.	-05	05	-10	-04	-03	24	11	11
E 7.	-09	01	-03	-11	07	-17	03	-13
E 8.	-02	-17	14	07	12	00	-18	01
E 9.	08	05	03	-10	-27	05	-02	-08
E 10.	04	17	-11	-12	16	00	04	-06
E 11.	04	17	-03	05	05	-09	-14	06
E 12.	-11	-18	10	10	12	15	09	-03
E 13.	11	22	-22	-05	08	-22	-08	-01
E 14.	-16	-08	17	-17	01	03	-10	-10
E 15.	-18	01	22	14	-24	11	08	-07
G 1.	-03	08	10	-13	-23	08	05	02

Table 13 (Continued)

		A 4	A 5	A 6	A 7	A 8	A 9	A 10	A 11	A 12
CC	1.									
CC	2.									
CC	3.									
CC	4.									
CC	5.									
CC	6.									
CC	7.									
CC	8.									
A	1.									
A	2.									
A	3.									
A	4.									
A	5.	43								
A	6.	29	46							
A	7.	27	-06	09						
A	8.	04	14	14	02					
A	9.	15	27	26	12	05				
A	10.	-10	-32	-20	-14	-01	-73			
A	11.	12	36	36	05	15	55	-44		
A	12.	-13	-44	-23	05	-15	-36	43	-83	
A	13.	07	03	20	21	09	28	-16	13	-02
A	14.	31	02	13	07	04	11	00	03	02
A	15.	23	17	16	18	01	26	-03	30	-25
A	16.	38	17	41	24	19	09	-06	07	00
E	1.	09	10	08	02	-16	07	06	11	-11
E	2.	-24	-30	-29	-07	15	-05	13	-28	22
E	3.	-05	-08	09	07	·15	17	-11	-11	17
E	4.	-04	06	-10	-15	-15	-11	23	-03	05
E	5.	-03	07	19	-09	-05	12	-21	14	-11
E	6.	31	16	14	13	-06	04	-05	02	-08
E	7.	-20	-08	-29	-11	21	-28	21	-06	-02
E	8.	06	01	12	-04	-13	-08	00	-16	19
E	9.	18	11	-07	15	-26	05	05	-05	12
E	10.	00	-06	-10	-02	06	01	-08	04	-10
E	11.	-10	-24	-01	07	-09	05	00	06	-07
E	12.	-08	08	30	-11	11	-10	08	05	-11
E	13.	03	06	-07	11	21	02	09	00	04
E	14.	17	26	08	01	-02	10	-18	14	-12
E	15.	-05	-17	-03	03	-11	-02	-11	09	00
G	1.	04	05	-08	28	-10	-17	04	-06	06

Table 13 (Continued)

	A 13	A 14	A 15	A 16	E 1	E 2	E 3	E 4
CC 1.								
CC 2.								
CC 3.								
CC 4.								
CC 5.								
CC 6.								
CC 7.								
CC 8.								
A 1.								
A 2.								
A 3.								
A 4.								
A 5.								
A 6.								
A 7.								
A 8.								
A 9.								
A 10.								
A 11.								
A 12.								
A 13.								
A 14.	26							
A 15.	19	18						
A 16.	30	39	29					
E 1.	03	09	12	-01				
E 2.	-01	-05	-18	00	-16			
E 3.	04	03	-17	18	-07	32		
E 4.	14	00	23	-09	26	-13	-22	
E 5.	18	09	-04	13	07	05	00	-02
E 6.	-07	20	11	11	07	-11	-32	-27
E 7.	-15	-23	-21	-08	-25	14	-14	-08
E 8.	-08	09	-04	-04	-22	-18	-16	-17
E 9.	10	18	10	02	15	-22	-24	24
E 10.	-07	-18	01	-23	-21	-04	14	-20
E 11.	-08	12	-01	-08	-13	-03	-03	-41
E 12.	-04	-02	17	08	02	-09	-23	11
E 13.	-26	-33	-02	-06	-11	09	22	-19
E 14.	07	-07	15	13	-06	-31	-26	22
E 15.	23	24	-14	-09	-04	-27	-11	05
G 1.	05	23	09	16	14	-01	02	05

Table 13 (Continued)

	E 5	E 6	E 7	E 8	E 9	E 10	E 11	E 12	E 13	E 14	E 15
CC1.											
CC2.											
CC3.											
CC4.											
CC5.											
CC6.											
CC7.											
CC8.											
A 1.											
A 2.											
A 3.											
A 4.											
A 5.											
A 6.											
A 7.											
A 8.											
A 9.											
A 10.											
A 11.											
A 12.											
A 13.											
A 14.											
A 15.											
A 16.											
E 1.											
E 2.											
E 3.											
E 4.											
E 5.											
E 6.	-12										
E 7.	-22	04									
E 8.	-10	08	-13								
E 9.	-10	01	-04	04							
E 10.	-20	06	-03	-14	-53						
E 11.	-13	39	-04	19	-23	18					
E 12.	16	06	-15	-03	-30	-08	-18				
E 13.	-18	-18	18	-30	01	13	-04	-11			
E 14.	-10	-26	-22	08	08	-05	-37	-01	-22		
E 15.	03	-26	-20	14	28	-24	-08	-13	-39	18	
G 1.	01	07	-08	-14	25	-18	-10	01	-20	03	17

RESULTS OF INTERBATTERY ANALYSIS

Table 14

UNROTATED INTERBATTERY FACTOR LOADINGS[a]

Score	I	II	III	h^2
		Factor		
CC 1. Embedded Figures: Mean Log Time	70	-11	09	51
CC 2. Rod and Frame: Average Error	44	-12	-27	28
CC 3. Color-Word: Interference	09	-16	-11	05
CC 4. Size Estimation: Constant Error	01	16	06	03
CC 5. Schematizing: Increment Error	-01	42	-13	19
CC 6. Schematizing: Ranking Accuracy	-16	-47	04	25
CC 7. Object Sorting: Number of Groups	19	06	50	29
CC 8. Size Constancy: Mean Diameter	35	17	-06	16
A 1. Concealed Figures: Number Correct	-86	-10	15	77
A 2. Designs: Number Correct	-48	03	-09	24
A 3. Spatial Orientation: Number Correct	-68	36	00	59
A 4. Cards: Number Correct	-39	11	-46	38
A 5. Wide Range Vocabulary: Number Correct	-42	-23	-22	28
A 6. Mathematics Aptitude: Number Correct	-30	-33	23	25
A 7. Thing Categories: Number of Words	-14	11	-30	12
A 8. Thing Categories: Percentage Round	-10	42	30	28
A 9. Picture-Number: Number Correct	-18	46	28	32
A 10. Picture-Number: Percentage Incorrect	-03	-17	-04	03
A 11. Word-Number: Number Correct	-52	27	25	41
A 12. Word-Number: Number Incorrect	41	-14	-19	22
A 13. Letter Grouping: Number Correct	-55	14	-22	38
A 14. Marks: Number Correct	-18	02	21	08
A 15. False Premises: Number Correct	-20	33	07	15
A 16. Reasoning: Number Correct	-14	16	02	05
E 1. Achievement	-37	-35	37	40
E 2. Deference	28	29	14	18
E 3. Order	21	38	20	23
E 4. Exhibition	-43	-21	-09	24
E 5. Autonomy	20	-09	32	15
E 6. Affiliation	07	08	-20	05
E 7. Intraception	04	-01	-27	07
E 8. Succorance	08	-28	09	09
E 9. Dominance	-21	-04	-14	07
E 10. Abasement	-02	33	-20	15
E 11. Nurturance	34	08	-09	13
E 12. Change	06	-24	18	09

[a]Decimal points omitted.

Table 14 (Continued)

| | Factor | | | |
	I	II	III	h^2
E 13. Endurance	08	44	-15	22
E 14. Heterosexuality	-22	-24	-23	16
E 15. Aggression	-16	-26	26	16
G 1. Home Index	-26	-11	-16	11
Percentage of Variance	11.1	6.2	4.7	22.0
Percentage of Common Variance	50.5	28.2	21.4	

Table 15

NORMAL VARIMAX ROTATION OF INTERBATTERY FACTORS

Transformation Matrix[a]

| | | Rotated | | |
		I	II	III
	I	74	10	66
Unrotated	II	-37	88	29
	III	-56	-46	69

[a]Decimal points omitted.

Table 16

NORMAL VARIMAX ROTATION OF INTERBATTERY

Factor Loadings[a]

Score	Factor I	II	III
CC1. Embedded Figures: Mean Log Time	51	-07	50
CC2. Rod and Frame: Average Error	52	06	07
CC3. Color-Word: Interference	19	-08	-06
CC4. Size Estimation: Constant Error	-08	11	10
CC5. Schematizing: Increment Error	-09	42	03
CC6. Schematizing: Ranking Accuracy	03	-44	-22
CC7. Object Sorting: Number of Groups	-16	-16	49
CC8. Size Constancy: Mean Diameter	23	21	24
A 1. Concealed Figures: Number Correct	-68	-24	-49
A 2. Designs: Number Correct	-32	03	-37
A 3. Spatial Orientation: Number Correct	-64	25	-34
A 4. Cards: Number Correct	-08	27	-54
A 5. Wide Range Vocabulary: Number Correct	-10	-14	-50
A 6. Mathematics Aptitude: Number Correct	-22	-43	-14
A 7. Thing Categories: Number of Words	02	22	-26
A 8. Thing Categories: Percentage Round	-40	22	26
A 9. Picture-Number: Number Correct	-46	26	21
A 10. Picture-Number: Percentage Incorrect	06	-13	-10
A 11. Word-Number: Number Correct	-63	08	-09
A 12. Word-Number: Percentage Incorrect	46	00	10
A 13. Letter Grouping: Number Correct	-34	17	-47
A 14. Marks: Number Correct	-26	-10	03
A 15. False Premises: Number Correct	-31	24	02
A 16. Reasoning: Number Correct	-18	12	-03
E 1. Achievement	-35	-52	-09
E 2. Deference	02	22	37
E 3. Order	-10	26	39
E 4. Exhibition	-19	-19	-41
E 5. Autonomy	00	-21	32
E 6. Affiliation	13	18	-06
E 7. Intraception	19	13	-16
E 8. Succorance	12	-28	03
E 9. Dominance	-06	00	-25
E 10. Abasement	-03	38	-06
E 11. Nurturance	27	15	19
E 12. Change	03	-29	10
E 13. Endurance	-02	46	08
E 14. Heterosexuality	06	-13	-37
E 15. Aggression	-17	-36	00
G 1. Home Index	-06	-04	-32
Percentage of Variance	8.4	5.9	7.6
Percentage of Common Variance	38.4	26.9	34.7

[a]Decimal points omitted.

APPENDIX C

RESULTS OF PRINCIPAL COMPONENTS ANALYSIS

Table 17

UNROTATED PRINCIPAL COMPONENTS FACTOR LOADINGS[a]

Score		I	II	III	IV	V	VI	h^2
				Factor				
CC1. Embedded Figures: Mean Log Time		-73	-25	-23	27	-09	-43	91
CC2. Rod and Frame: Average Error		-45	-07	-37	09	05	06	36
CC3. Color-Word: Interference		-06	45	-03	01	17	00	24
CC4. Size Estimation: Constant Error		05	03	09	03	14	-32	13
CC5. Schematizing: Increment Error		00	-56	09	-44	22	00	56
CC6. Schematizing: Ranking Accuracy		09	36	08	05	-18	02	18
CC7. Object Sorting: Number of Groups		-17	-35	30	17	-58	01	61
CC8. Size Constancy: Mean Diameter		-33	-38	-03	02	36	03	39
A 1. Concealed Figures: Number Correct		76	20	01	-20	-21	-11	71
A 2. Designs: Number Correct		37	23	10	-17	04	-22	28
A 3. Spatial Orientation: Number Correct		61	-09	04	-16	00	06	41
A 4. Cards: Number Correct		53	01	-45	07	22	00	54

[a]Decimal points omitted.

132

Table 17 (Continued)

Score			Factor				h^2
	I	II	III	IV	V	VI	
A 5. Wide Range Vocabulary: Number Correct	47	08	-05	50	29	13	58
A 6. Mathematics Aptitude: Number Correct	56	04	-10	45	-12	-02	54
A 7. Thing Categories: Number of Words	19	-13	-25	-12	09	06	14
A 8. Thing Categories: Percentage Round	13	-38	06	14	-10	48	42
A 9. Picture-Number: Number Correct	44	-35	27	18	16	-27	52
A 11. Word-Number: Number Correct	53	-20	42	24	14	-06	58
A 13. Letter Grouping: Number Correct	47	-07	-03	-29	-05	-01	31
A 14. Marks: Number Correct	31	-15	-26	-10	-29	-14	30
A 15. False Premises: Number Correct	35	-30	-05	00	06	-11	23
A 16. Reasoning: Number Correct	49	-28	-50	04	-23	-03	62
Percentage of Variance	18.2	7.3	5.3	4.9	4.6	3.3	43.6
Percentage of Common Variance	41.7	16.7	12.2	11.2	10.6	7.6	

Table 18

NORMAL VARIMAX ROTATION OF
PRINCIPAL COMPONENTS FACTORS
Transformation Matrix[a]

		Rotated					
		I	II	III	IV	V	VI
	I	74	09	-49	44	11	00
	II	10	79	29	-12	49	-15
Unrotated	III	52	-08	73	07	-41	-10
	IV	-41	27	12	83	-22	02
	V	-02	-53	29	31	71	-21
	VI	07	00	18	04	19	96

[a]Decimal points omitted.

Table 19

NORMAL VARIMAX ROTATION OF PRINCIPAL COMPONENTS FACTORS

Factor Loadings[a]

Score	Factor					
	I	II	III	IV	V	VI
CC1. Embedded Figures: Mean Log Time	-83	-12	05	-12	-31	-33
CC2. Rod and Frame: Average Error	-57	-07	-03	-13	09	10
CC3. Color-Word: Interference	-02	27	19	-02	34	-10
CC4. Size Estimation: Constant Error	05	-04	04	08	02	-35
CC5. Schematizing: Increment Error	17	-68	-08	-23	-06	02
CC6. Schematizing: Ranking Accuracy	13	40	08	-01	02	-01
CC7. Object Sorting: Number of Groups	-06	04	05	-04	-76	15
CC8. Size Constancy: Mean Diameter	-31	-51	14	03	04	02
A 1. Concealed Figures: Number Correct	66	28	-41	08	05	-09
A 2. Designs: Number Correct	40	14	-09	00	13	-27
A 3. Spatial Orientation: Number Correct	53	-07	-31	15	05	07
A 4. Cards: Number Correct	13	-01	-52	32	38	00
A 5. Wide Range Vocabulary: Number Correct	12	10	-08	70	23	07

[a]Decimal points omitted.

Table 19 (Continued)

Score		Factor				
	I	II	III	IV	V	VI
A 6. Mathematics Aptitude: Number Correct	18	28	-32	57	-06	02
A 7. Thing Categories: Number of Words	05	-15	-29	01	16	08
A 8. Thing Categories: Percentage Round	07	-21	-05	21	-21	54
A 9. Picture-Number: Number Correct	33	-30	-10	45	-21	-27
A 11. Word-Number: Number Correct	48	-16	05	53	-18	-09
A 13. Letter Grouping: Number Correct	44	-06	-32	-04	05	01
A 14. Marks: Number Correct	12	06	-51	-04	-14	-03
A 15. False Premises: Number Correct	20	-23	-30	21	-06	-07
A 16. Reasoning: Number Correct	06	-01	-76	17	-05	11
Percentage of Variance	12.3	6.4	8.4	7.5	5.5	3.5
Percentage of Common Variance	28.2	14.7	19.3	17.2	12.6	8.0

Table 20

OBLIMAX ROTATION OF PRINCIPAL
COMPONENT FACTORS

Transformation Matrix from Varimax Position to Oblimax Position[a]

| | | Oblimax | | | | | |
		I	II	III	IV	V	VI
	I	91	-21	29	-10	-06	03
	II	20	96	-08	-05	-20	-11
Varimax	III	20	-02	95	15	-03	10
	IV	-25	03	00	98	06	17
	V	17	-03	08	11	95	-12
	VI	03	18	-05	00	-21	97

[a]Decimal points omitted.

Table 21

OBLIMAX ROTATION OF PRINCIPAL COMPONENTS FACTORS

Reference Factor Structure[a]

Score		Factor				
	I	II	III	IV	V	VI
CC1. Embedded Figures: Mean Log Time	-80	00	-19	-06	-16	-32
CC2. Rod and Frame: Average Error	-48	06	-19	-06	11	04
CC3. Color-Word: Interference	14	23	18	03	29	-16
CC4. Size Estimation: Constant Error	02	-11	07	08	10	-31
CC5. Schematizing: Increment Error	05	-69	02	-23	06	06
CC6. Schematizing: Ranking Accuracy	22	35	08	-02	-07	-04
CC7. Object Sorting: Number of Groups	-15	10	-04	-11	-76	23
CC8. Size Constancy: Mean Diameter	-36	-43	09	11	16	08
A 1. Concealed Figures: Number Correct	56	12	-21	-06	-01	-13

Table 21 (Continued)

Score	Factor					
	I	II	III	IV	V	VI
A 2. Designs: Number Correct	39	00	05	-05	13	-28
A 3. Spatial Orientation: Number Correct	38	-15	-13	06	03	08
A 4. Cards: Number Correct	00	-02	-42	26	39	-03
A 5. Wide Range Vocabulary: Number Correct	-02	09	-03	68	22	14
A 6. Mathematics Aptitude: Number Correct	00	26	-28	47	-09	06
A 7. Thing Categories: Number of Words	-02	-13	-24	-02	17	05
A 8. Thing Categories: Percentage Round	-07	-10	-06	18	-26	60
A 9. Picture-Number: Number Correct	06	-38	03	38	-08	-12
A 11. Word-Number: Number Correct	25	-25	19	46	-12	06
A 13. Letter Grouping: Number Correct	34	-15	-17	-13	04	-01
A 14. Marks: Number Correct	00	04	-47	-15	-13	-07
A 15. False Premises: Number Correct	01	-26	-21	14	01	-02
A 16. Reasoning: Number Correct	-15	02	-71	04	-04	07

[a]Decimal points omitted.

Table 22

OBLIMAX ROTATION OF PRINCIPAL
COMPONENTS FACTORS

Primary Factor Correlations[a]

	I	II	III	IV	V	VI
I	100	-13	-53	42	-14	-07
II	-13	100	21	-11	25	02
III	-53	21	100	-31	07	00
IV	42	-11	-31	100	-27	-24
V	-14	25	07	-27	100	33
VI	-07	02	00	-24	33	100

[a]Decimal points omitted.

BIBLIOGRAPHY

Adkins, D. C. & Lyerly, S. B. (1952), *Factor Analysis of Reasoning Tests.* Chapel Hill: University of North Carolina.

Anthony, J. (1957), The System Makers: Piaget and Freud. In Symposium on the Contribution of Current Theories to an Understanding of Child Development. *Brit. J. Med. Psychol.,* 30:255-269.

Barratt, E. S. (1953), An Analysis of Verbal Reports of Solving Spatial Problems As an Aid in Defining Spatial Factors. *J. Psychol.,* 36:17-25.

———— (1955),The Space-Visualization Factors Related to Temperament Traits. *J. Psychol.,* 39:279-287.

Bartlett, F. C. (1932), *Remembering: A Study in Experimental and Social Psychology.* Cambridge: Cambridge University Press.

Bergson, H. (1911), *Matter and Memory.* London: Allen & Unwin.

Bieri, J., Bradburn, W. M., & Galinsky, M. D. (1958), Sex Differences in Perceptual Behavior. *J. Pers.,* 26:1-12.

Bruner, J. S., Goodnow, J., & Austin, G. A. (1956), *A Study of Thinking.* New York: Wiley.

Cattell, R. B. (1945), Personality Traits Associated with Abilities. II: With Verbal and Mathematical Abilities. *J. Educ. Psychol.,* 36:475-486.

———— (1955), The Principal Replicated Factors Discovered in Objective Personality Tests. *J. Abn. Soc. Psychol.,* 50:291-314.

———— (1957), *Personality and Motivation Structure and Measurement.* Yonkers-on-Hudson: World Book.

Clayton, M. & Jackson, D. N. (In press), Equivalence Range, Acquiescence, and Overgeneralization. *Educ. Psychol. Measmt.*

Crutchfield, R. S., Woodworth, D. G., & Albrecht, R. E. (1958), Perceptual Performance and the Effective Person. Armed Services Technical Information Agency, Document No. AD 151039.

Dickman, N. R. (1954), An Investigation of the Relationship Between the Cognitive Organization of Objective and Behavioral Stimuli. Unpublished master's thesis. On file, University of Kansas library.

Duncker, K. (1935), On Problem Solving. *Psychol. Monogr.,* 58 (5), 1945.

Edwards, A. L. (1954), *Manual* for Edwards Personal Preference Schedule. New York: The Psychological Corp.

Eysenck, H. J., Granger, G. W., & Brengelmann, J. C. (1957), *Perceptual Processes and Mental Illness.* New York: Basic Books.

Fraisse, P., Ehrlich, S., & Vurpillot, E. (1956), Études de la centration perceptive par la méthode tachistoscopique. *Arch. Psychol.,* Genève, 35:193-214.

Frederiksen, N., & Messick, S. (1959), Response Set As a Measure of Personality. *Educ. Psychol. Measmt.,* 19:137-158.

French, J. W. (1951), *The Description of Aptitude and Achievement Tests in Terms of Rotated Factors.* Psychometric Monogr. No. 5. Chicago: University of Chicago Press.

141

———— Ed. (1954), *Manual for Kit of Selected Tests for Reference Aptitude and Achievement Factors.* Princeton: Educational Testing Service.

Freud, A. (1936), *The Ego and the Mechanisms of Defence.* New York: International Universities Press, 1946.

Freud, S. (1895), Project for a Scientific Psychology. In *The Origins of Psychoanalysis, Letters to Wilhelm Fliess, Drafts and Notes: 1887-1902.* New York: Basic Books, 1954, pp. 347-445.

———— (1900), The Interpretation of Dreams. *Standard Edition,* Vols. 4 & 5. London: Hogarth Press, 1953.

———— (1911), Formulations on the Two Principles of Mental Functioning. *Standard Edition,* 12:213-226. London: Hogarth Press, 1958.

———— (1915a), Repression. *Standard Edition,* 14:146-158. London: Hogarth Press, 1957.

———— (1915b), The Unconscious. *Standard Edition.* 14:166-215. London: Hogarth Press, 1957.

———— (1923), *The Ego and the Id.* London: Hogarth Press, 1947.

———— (1925a), A Note Upon the "Mystic Writing-Pad." *Collected Papers,* 5:175-180. London: Hogarth Press, 1950.

———— (1925b), Negation. *Collected Papers,* 5:181-185. London: Hogarth Press, 1950.

———— (1926), Inhibitions, Symptoms and Anxiety. *Standard Edition,* 20:77-175. London: Hogarth Press, 1959.

———— (1937), Analysis Terminable and Interminable. *Collected Papers,* 5:316-357. London: Hogarth Press, 1950.

Fruchter, B. (1954), Measurement of Spatial Abilities: History and Background. *Educ. Psychol. Measmt.,* 14:387-395.

Gardner, R. W. (1953), Cognitive Styles in Categorizing Behavior. *J. Pers.,* 22:214-233.

———— (1957), Field Dependence as a Determinant of Susceptibility to Certain Illusions (Abstract). *Amer. Psychologist,* 12:397.

———— (1959), Cognitive Control Principles and Perceptual Behavior. *Bull. Menninger Clin.,* 23:241-248.

———— (1960), Cognitive Controls in Adaptation: A Strategy for Current Research. Paper presented at Conference on Personality Measurement, Educational Testing Service, Princeton, New Jersey.

———— (In press), Cognitive Controls of Attention Deployment as Determinants of Visual Illusions. *J. Abn. Soc. Psychol.*

———— & Holzman, P. S., Klein, G. S., Linton, H. B., Spence, D. (1959), Cognitive Control: A Study of Individual Consistencies in Cognitive Behavior. *Psychological Issues,* 1 (4). New York: International Universities Press.

———— & Jackson, D. N., Messick, S. (1958), Personality Organization in Cognitive Attitudes and Intellectual Abilities (Abstract). *Amer. Psychologist,* 13:336.

———— & Klein, G. S., Schlesinger, H. J. (1951), Perceptual Attitudes Toward Instability: Prediction from Apparent Movement Responses to Other Tasks Involving Resolution of Unstable Fields (Abstract). *Amer. Psychologist,* 6:332.

———— & Lohrenz, L. J. (1960), Leveling-Sharpening and Serial Reproduction of a Story. *Bull. Menninger Clin.,* 24:295-304.

———— & ———— (In preparation), Attention and Assimilation.

———— & Long, R. I. (1960a), Errors of the Standard and Illusion Effects with the Inverted-*T. Percept. Mot. Skills,* 10:47-54.

———— & ———— (1960b), Errors of the Standard and Illusion Effects with *L*-Shaped Figures. *Percept. Mot. Skills,* 10:107-109.

———— & ———— (1960c), Cognitive Controls in Learning and Recall. Paper presented at Annual Meeting of Southwestern Psychological Association, Galveston, Texas.

———— & ———— (1960d), Leveling-Sharpening and Serial Learning. *Percept. Mot. Skills,* 10:179-185.

———— & ———— (In press), The Stability of Cognitive Controls. *J. Abn. Soc. Psychol.*

———— & ———— (In preparation, a), Field-Articulation in recall.

———— & ———— (In preparation, b), Cognitive Controls in Scanning Behaviors.

———— & ———— (In preparation, c), Cognitive Controls in Field-Articulation and Scanning.

Gehlmann, F. (1951), Performance on Objective Tests as Indicators of Temperament and Other Personality Traits. Unpublished doctoral dissertation. On file, University of Chicago library.

Gollin, E. S. & Baron, A. (1954), Response Consistency in Perception and Retention. *J. Exp. Psychol.,* 47:259-262.

Gottschaldt, K. (1926, 1929), Über den Einfluss der Erfahrung auf die Wahrnehmung von Figuren. I & II. *Psychol. Forsch.,* 8:261-317; 12:1-87.

Gough, H. B. (1949), A Short Social Status Inventory. *J. Educ. Psychol.,* 40:52-56.

Guilford, J. P. (1940), Human Abilities. *Psychol. Rev.,* 47:367-394.

———— Ed. (1947), *Printed Classification Tests, AAF Report No. 5.* Washington, D.C.: U.S. Government Printing Office.

———— (1950), Creativity. *Amer. Psychologist,* 5:444-454.

———— (1956), The Structure of Intellect. *Psychol. Bull.,* 53:267-293.

———— (1959a), *Personality.* New York: McGraw-Hill.

———— (1959b), Three Faces of Intellect. *Amer. Psychologist,* 14:469-479.

———— & Christensen, P. R., Kettner, N. W., Hertska, A. F. (1954), A Factor-Analytic Study of Navy Reasoning Tests with the Air Force Aircrew Classification Battery. *Educ. Psychol. Measmt.,* 14:301-325.

———— & Frick, J. W., Christensen, P. R., Merrifield, P. R. (1957), A Factor-Analytic Study of Flexibility in Thinking. *Rep. Psychol. Lab., No. 18.* Los Angeles: University of Southern California.

———— & Green, R. F., Christensen, P. R. (1951), A Factor-Analytic Study of Reasoning Abilities. II. Administration of Tests and Analysis of Results. *Rep. Psychol. Lab., No. 3.* Los Angeles: University of Southern California.

———— & Kettner, N. W., Christensen, P. R. (1955), A Factor-Analytic Investigation of the Factor Called General Reasoning. *Rep. Psychol. Lab., No. 14.* Los Angeles: University of Southern California.

Hartmann, H. (1939), *Ego Psychology and the Problem of Adaptation,* tr. D. Rapaport. New York: International Universities Press, 1958.

———— (1950), Comments on the Psychoanalytic Theory of the Ego. *The Psychoanalytic Study of the Child,* 5:74-96. New York: International Universities Press.

———— (1956), The Development of the Ego Concept in Freud's Work. *Int. J. Psychoanal.,* 37:425-437.

———— & Kris, E. (1945), The Genetic Approach in Psychoanalysis. *The Psychoanalytic Study of the Child,* 1:11-29. New York: International Universities Press.

———— ———— & Loewenstein, R. M. (1946), Comments on the Formation of Psychic Structure. *The Psychoanalytic Study of the Child,* 2:11-38. New York: International Universities Press.

Hebb, D. O. (1949), *Organization of Behavior.* New York: Wiley.

Hollingworth, H. (1913), The Central Tendency of Judgment in Experimental Studies of Judgment. *Arch. Psychol.,* 29:44-52.

Holzman, P. S. (1954), The Relation of Assimilation Tendencies in Visual, Auditory, and Kinesthetic Time-Error to Cognitive Attitudes of Leveling and Sharpening, *J. Pers.,* 22:375-394.

—— (1960), Repression and Cognitive Style. In *Festschrift for Gardner Murphy,* ed. J. G. Peatman & E. L. Hartley. New York: Harper.

—— & Gardner, R. W. (1959), Leveling and Repression. *J. Abn. Soc. Psychol.,* 59:151-155.

—— & —— (In press), Leveling-Sharpening and Memory Organization. *J. Abn. Soc. Psychol.*

—— & Klein, G. S. (1954), Cognitive System-Principles of Leveling and Sharpening: Individual Differences in Assimilation Effects in Visual Time-Error. *J. Psychol.,* 37:105-122.

—— & —— (1956), Motive and Style in Reality Contact. *Bull. Menninger Clin.,* 20:181-191.

Jackson, D. N. (1955), Stability in Resistance to Field Forces. Unpublished doctoral dissertation. On file, Purdue University library.

—— (1957), Intellectual Ability and Mode of Perception. *J. Consult. Psychol.,* 21:458.

—— & Messick, S. J. (1958), Content and Style in Personaltiy Assessment. *Psychol. Bull.,* 55:243-252.

Jay, R. L. (1950), The Relation Between Some Perceptual Factors and Some Personality Categories. Unpublished master's thesis. On file, University of Chicago.

Kaiser, H. F. (1958), The Varimax Criterion for Analytic Rotation in Factor Analysis. *Psychometrika,* 23:187-200.

Klein, G. S. (1949a), Adaptive Properties of Sensory Functioning: Some Postulates and Hypotheses. *Bull. Menninger Clin.,* 13:16-23.

—— (1949b), A Clinical Perspective for Personality Research. *J. Abn. Soc. Psychol.,* 44:42-50.

—— (1951), The Personal World Through Perception. In *Perception: An Approach to Personality,* ed. R. R. Blake & G. V. Ramsey. New York: Ronald Press.

—— (1953), The Menninger Foundation Research on Perception and Personality, 1947-1952: A Review. *Bull. Menninger Clin.,* 17:93-99.

—— (1954), Need and Regulation. In *Nebraska Symposium on Motivation,* ed. M. R. Jones. Lincoln: University of Nebraska Press, pp. 224-280.

—— (1956), Perception, Motives and Personality: A Clinical Perspective. In *Psychology of Personality,* ed. J. L. McCary. New York: Logos.

—— (1958), Cognitive Control and Motivation. In *Assessment of Human Motives,* ed. G. Lindzey. New York: Rinehart.

—— (1959), Consciousness in Psychoanalytic Theory: Some Implications for Current Research in Perception. *J. Amer. Psa. Assn.,* 7:5-34.

—— & Gardner, R. W., Schlesinger, H. J. (In press), Tolerance for Unrealistic Experiences: A Generality Study. *Brit. J. Psychol.*

—— & Holzman, P. S., Laskin, D. (1954), The Perception Project: Progress Report for 1953-54. *Bull. Menninger Clin.,* 18:260-266.

—— & Schlesinger, H. J. (1949), Where Is the Perceiver in Perceptual Theory? *J. Pers.,* 18:32-47.

—— & —— (1951), Perceptual Attitudes Toward Instability: I. Prediction of Apparent Movement Experiences from Rorschach Responses. *J. Pers.,* 19:289-302.

Klüver, H. (1936), The Study of Personality and the Method of Equivalent and Non-Equivalent Stimuli. *Charact. & Pers.,* 5:91-112.

Koffka, K. (1935), *Principles of Gestalt Psychology.* New York: Harcourt, Brace.

Köhler, W. (1923), Zur Theorie des Sukzessivvergleichs und der Zeitfehler. *Psychol. Forsch.,* 4:115-175.

—— (1958), Perceptual Organization and Learning. *Amer. J. Psychol.*, 71:311-315.

—— & Adams, P. A. (1958), Perception and Attention. *Amer. J. Psychol.*, 71:489-503.

Krathwohl, D. R. & Cronbach, L. J. (1956), Suggestions Regarding a Possible Measure of Personality: The Squares Test. *Educ. Psychol. Measmt.*, 16:305-316.

Krech, D. & Calvin, A. D. (1953), Levels of Perceptual Organization and Cognition. *J. Abn. Soc. Psychol.*, 48:394-400.

Lacey, J. I. (1956), The Evaluation of Autonomic Responses: Toward a General Solution. *Ann. N.Y. Acad. Sci.*, 67:123-164.

Lambercier, M. (1946a), La constance des grandeurs en comparaisons sériales. *Arch. Psychol.*, Genève, 31:79-282.

—— (1946b), La configuration en profondeur dans la constance des grandeurs. *Arch. Psychol.*, Genève, 31:287-324.

Lauenstein, O. (1933), Ansatz zu einer physiologischen Theorie des Vergleichs und der Zeitfehler. *Psychol. Forsch.*, 17:130-177.

Lewin, K. (1935), *A Dynamic Theory of Personality*. New York: McGraw-Hill.

Linton, H. B. (1955), Dependence on External Influence: Correlates in Perception, Attitudes and Judgment. *J. Abn. Soc. Psychol.*, 51:502-507.

—— & Graham, E. (1959), Personality Correlates of Persuasibility. In *Personality and Persuasibility*, ed. C. I. Hovland. New Haven: Yale University Press.

Lord, F. M. (1956), The Measurement of Growth. *Educ. Psychol. Measmt.*, 16:421-437.

Marrs, C. L. (1955), Categorizing Behavior As Elicited by a Variety of Stimuli. Unpublished master's thesis. On file, University of Kansas library.

Mathae, D. E. (1958), Figural Aftereffects, Weight Judgment and Schematizing in Relation to "Cortical Conductivity." Unpublished doctoral dissertation. On file, University of Kansas library.

Michael, W. G. (1954), A Suggested Research Approach to the Identification of Psychological Processes Associated with Spatial-Visualization Factors. *Educ. Psychol. Measmt.*, 14:401-406.

—— & Guilford, J. P., Fruchter, B., Zimmerman, W. S. (1957), The Description of Spatial-Visualization Abilities. *Educ. Psychol. Measmt.*, 17:185-199.

Murphy, G. (1947), *Personality*. New York: Harper.

Murray, H. A. et al. (1938), *Explorations in Personality*. New York: Oxford University Press.

Nunberg, H. (1931), The Synthetic Function of the Ego. *Int. J. Psychoanal.*, 12:123-140.

Paul, I. H. (1959), Studies in Remembering: The Reproduction of Connected and Extended Verbal Material. *Psychological Issues*, 1 (2). New York: International Universities Press.

Pemberton, C. L. (1952a), The Closure Factors Related to Other Cognitive Processes. *Psychometrika*, 17:267-288.

—— (1952b), The Closure Factors Related to Temperament. *J. Pers.*, 21:159-175.

Pettigrew, T. F. (1958), The Measurement and Correlates of Category Width As a Cognitive Variable. *J. Pers.*, 26:532-544.

Piaget, J. (1936), *The Origins of Intelligence in Children*, tr. M. Cook. New York: International Universities Press, 1952.

—— (1947), *The Psychology of Intelligence*, tr. M. Piercy & D. E. Berlyne. London: Routledge & Kegan Paul, 1950.

—— (1950), Perception et intelligence. *Bull. Gr. Étud. Psychol.*, University of Paris, 4:25-34.

———— & Lambercier, M. (1943a), La comparaison visuelle des hauteurs à distances variables dans le plan fronto-parallèle. *Arch. Psychol.*, Genève, 29:173-253.

———— & ———— (1943b), Le problème de la comparaison visuelle en profondeur (constance de la grandeur) et l'erreur systématique de l'étalon. *Arch. Psychol.*, Genève, 29:255-308.

———— & ———— (1951), La comparaison des grandeurs projectives chez l'enfant et chez l'adulte. *Arch. Psychol.*, Genève, 33:81-130.

———— & ———— (1956), Grandeurs projectives et grandeurs réelles avec étalon éloigné. *Arch. Psychol.*, Genève, 35:257-280.

———— & Vinh-Bang, Matalon, B. (1958), Note on the Law of the Temporal Maximum of Some Optico-Geometric Illusions. *Amer. J. Psychol.*, 71:277-282.

———— & von Albertini, B. (1950), L'illusion de Müller-Lyer. *Arch. Psychol.*, Genève, 33:1-48.

Pinzka, C. & Saunders, D. R. (1954), Analytic Rotation to Simple Structure, II. Extension to an Oblique Solution. *Educ. Testing Serv. Bull.*, RB-54-31.

Podell, J. E. & Phillips, L. (1959), A Developmental Analysis of Cognition As Observed in Dimensions of Rorschach and Objective Test Performance. *J. Pers.*, 27:439-463.

Rapaport, D. (1942a), Principles Underlying Projective Techniques. *Charact. & Pers.*, 10:213-219.

———— (1942b), *Emotions and Memory.* New York: International Universities Press, 1950.

———— (1946), Principles Underlying Non-Projective Tests of Personality. *Ann. N.Y. Acad. Sci.*, 66:643-652.

———— (1950a), On the Psycho-Analytic Theory of Thinking. *Int. J. Psychoanal.*, 31:161-170.

———— (1950b), The Theoretical Implications of Diagnostic Testing Procedures. In *Congrès International de Psychiatrie*, 2:241-271. Paris: Hermann.

———— Ed. (1951a), *Organization and Pathology of Thought.* New York: Columbia University Press.

———— (1951b), The Autonomy of the Ego. *Bull. Menninger Clin.*, 15:113-123.

———— (1951c), The Conceptual Model of Psychoanalysis. *J. Pers.*, 20:56-81.

———— (1952), Projective Techniques and the Theory of Thinking. *J. Proj. Tech.*, 16:269-275.

———— (1953), Some Metapsychological Considerations Concerning Activity and Passivity. Unpublished ms.

———— (1957), Cognitive Structures. In *Contemporary Approaches to Cognition.* Cambridge: Harvard University Press, pp. 157-200.

———— (1958), The Theory of Ego Autonomy: A Generalization. *Bull. Menninger Clin.*, 22:13-35.

———— (1960a), The Structure of Psychoanalytic Theory: A Systematizing Attempt. *Psychological Issues*, 2 (2). New York: International Universities Press.

———— (1960b), On the Psychoanalytic Theory of Motivation. In *Nebraska Symposium on Motivation*, ed. M. R. Jones. Lincoln: University of Nebraska Press, pp. 173-247.

———— & Gill, M., Schafer, R. (1945, 1946), *Diagnostic Psychological Testing*, 2 Vols. Chicago: Yearbook Publ.

Rokeach, M. (1960), *The Open and Closed Mind.* New York: Basic Books.

Rudin, S. A. & Stagner, R. (1958), Figure-Ground Phenomena in the Perception of Physical and Social Stimuli. *J. Psychol.*, 45:213-225.

Schachtel, E. G. (1959), *Metamorphosis.* New York: Basic Books.

Schafer, R. (1948), *The Clinical Application of Psychological Tests.* New York: International Universities Press.

—— (1954), *Psychoanalytic Interpretation in Rorschach Testing*. New York: Grune & Stratton.

Scott, T. H., Bexton, W. H., Heron, W., & Doane, B. K. (1959), Cognitive Effects of Perceptual Isolation. *Canad. J. Psychol.,* 13:200-209.

Siegal, R. S. (1957), The Leveling-Sharpening System Principle, Serial Learning and Retroactive Interference. Unpublished doctoral dissertation. On file, University of Kansas library.

Sloane, H. N. (1959), The Generality and Construct Validity of Equivalence Range. Unpublished doctoral dissertation. On file, Pennsylvania State University library.

—— & Gorlow, L., Jackson, D. N. (In preparation), The Generality and Construct Validity of Equivalence Range.

Smith, F. E. (1951), Word Reactions and Temperament. Unpublished doctoral dissertation. On file, University of Chicago library.

Smith, G. J. W. & Klein, G. S. (1953), Cognitive Controls in Serial Behavior Patterns. *J. Pers.,* 22:188-213.

—— & Nyman, G. E. (1959), Psychopathologic Behavior in a Serial Experiment. Investigations of Neurotic, Psychotic, Psychopathic, and Normal Subjects. *Lunds Universitets Arsskrift. N. F.,* Avd. 2. 56, 5. Lund: Gleerup.

Spearman, C. (1927), *The Abilities of Man*. New York: Macmillan.

—— & Jones, W. L. (1951), *Human Ability*. London: Macmillan.

Spivack, G., Levine, M., & Sprigle, H. (1959), Intelligence Test Performance and the Delay Function of the Ego. *J. Consult. Psychol.,* 23:428-431.

Stroop, J. R. (1935), Studies in Interference in Serial Verbal Reaction. *J. Exp. Psychol.,* 18:643-661.

Thouless, R. H. (1931), Phenomenal Regression to the 'Real' Object. I. *Brit. J. Psychol.,* 21:339-359.

—— (1932a), Phenomenal Regression to the 'Real' Object. II. *Brit. J. Psychol.,* 22:1-30.

—— (1932b), Individual Differences in Phenomenal Regression. *Brit. J. Psychol.,* 22:216-241.

Thurstone, L. L. (1938), *Primary Mental Abilities*. Psychometric Monogr. No. 1. Chicago: University of Chicago Press.

—— (1944), *A Factorial Study of Perception*. Psychometric Monogr. No. 4. Chicago: University of Chicago Press.

—— (1947), *Multiple-Factor Analysis*. Chicago: University of Chicago Press.

—— (1948), Psychological Implications of Factor Analysis. *Amer. Psychologist,* 3:402-408.

—— (1950), Some Primary Abilities in Visual Thinking. *Psychometric Lab. Report No. 5*. Chicago: University of Chicago Press.

—— & Thurstone, T. G. (1941), *Factorial Studies of Intelligence*. Psychometric Monogr. No. 2. Chicago: University of Chicago Press.

Tomkins, S. S. (1951), Personality and Intelligence: Integration of Projective and Psychometric Techniques. In *Relation of Psychological Tests to Psychiatry*, ed. P. H. Hoch & J. Zubin. New York: Grune & Stratton.

Tucker, L. R (1958), An Inter-Battery Method of Factor Analysis. *Psychometrika,* 23:111-136.

Vernon, P. E. (1950), *The Structure of Human Abilities*. New York: Wiley.

Wechsler, D. (1958), *The Measurement of Adult Intelligence*, 4th ed. Baltimore: Williams and Wilkins.

Wertheim, J. & Mednick, S. A. (1958), The Achievement Motive and Field Independence. *J. Consult. Psychol.,* 22:38.

Witkin, H. A. (1949), The Nature and Importance of Individual Differences in Perception. *J. Pers.,* 18:145-170.

—— (1950), Individual Differences in Ease of Perception of Embedded Figures. *J. Pers.,* 19:1-15.

———— (1959), The Perception of the Upright. *Sci. Amer.*, 200:50-56.
———— & Karp, S. A., Goodenough, D. R. (1959), Dependence in Alcoholics. *Quart. J. Stud. Alc.*, 20:493-504.
———— & Lewis, H. B., Hertzman, M., Machover, K., Meissner, P. B., Wapner, S. (1954), *Personality Through Perception.* New York: Harper.
Wolff, P. H. (1960), The Developmental Psychologies of Jean Piaget and Psychoanalysis. *Psychological Issues,* 2 (1). New York: International Universities Press.
Yacorzynski, G. (1941), An Evaluation of the Postulates Underlying the Babcock Deterioration Test. *Psychol. Rev.,* 48:261-267.
Zimmerman, W. S. (1954a), The Influence of Item Complexity upon the Factor Composition of a Spatial Visualization Test. *Educ. Psychol. Measmt.,* 14:106-119.
———— (1954b), Hypotheses Concerning the Nature of the Spatial Factors. *Educ. Psychol. Measmt.,* 14:396-400.

About the Authors

Riley W. Gardner received his Ph.D. in psychology from the University of Kansas in 1952. He received his training in clinical psychology at Winter Veterans Administration Hospital and at The Menninger Foundation. He has been a member of The Menninger Foundation staff since 1951, and is director of the research group engaged in studying cognitive control principles.

Douglas N. Jackson received his Ph.D. in psychology from Purdue University. He received training in clinical psychology from the Veterans Administration. He was on the research staff of The Menninger Foundation, 1952 and 1953, where he served again in 1955 and 1956 as a Public Health Service Postdoctoral Fellow in Clinical Research. Since 1956 he has been an Assistant Professor of Psychology and a member of the Graduate Faculty at Pennsylvania State University.

Samuel Messick received his Ph.D. in psychology from Princeton University in 1954. From 1951 to 1954 he was an Educational Testing Service Psychometric Fellow. In 1954 he received a Ford Foundation Postdoctoral Fellowship for Research in Personality Dynamics and Development at the University of Illinois, and in 1955 he was a United States Public Health Service Fellow in Clinical Research at The Menninger Foundation. He has been a member of the research staff at Educational Testing Service since 1956, and is at present Chairman of the Personality Research Group.

149

B 2756

St. Patrick's Seminary Library

10000000035938

50627

BF 698 .G29 1960
Gardner, Riley Wetherell.
Personality organization

Gellert Memorial Library
St. Patrick's Seminary & University
320 Middlefield Rd.
Menlo Park, CA 94025
library.stpsu.edu

DISCARD